THE TOMBOY & THE MOVIE STAR

A JACKSON HIGH NOVEL

M.L. COLLINS

Editing by K&T Editing

Cover Design by NPTB Creatives

Made in the United States of America

Find out about M.L.'s next release!

Sign up for M.L. Collins's Newsletter!

This one's for the tomboys, the misfits, the girls who don't "fit in."
The girls who dare to be different.
#GirlMechanics #GirlsWhoWorkOnCars #FemaleMechanic
#BlueCollar #CarGirl #TechSchool

This book is also dedicated to my father who passed away while I was
writing this book. I was blessed with a wonderful dad. The laughter
and unconditional love he gave me are the bedrock I've built my
life on.
I love you, Dad.

PROLOGUE

Kingsly Grant

Have you ever had a jolt of intuition that you must do something, or else?

"This is Caitlyn Reed from WJSA reporting from the halls of Jackson High School. We're here getting reactions from students about the news that Hollywood's biggest teen heart-throb might film his next big blockbuster hit here." The reporter held a microphone in front of a group of giggling girls. "How do you feel about the possibility of Kingsly Grant coming to Jackson High to make his next movie?"

"OhmygoshOhmygoshOhmygosh! I'm pretty sure I'll faint if I see Kingsly Grant walking through the halls." The girl squealed into the microphone. "He's soooo hot!"

"Eeek! Then he could give you mouth-to-mouth resuscitation!" A girl standing next to her said. "I'm totally going to faint too."

"Me too!" Another girl grabbed the microphone. "You have to pick our school, King! We love you!"

The reporter proceeded to interview more female students, all of whom were over-the-top excited about the idea.

1

"See what we mean, King? The publicity during the selection process for the filming location is already through the roof." Frank, my agent since I'd started in this business at the age of eight, nodded across the table. "Donna, the idea of letting King pick the school was genius."

"I agree," I said. "But they don't call Donna the queen of publicity for nothing."

Donna snorted and rolled her eyes. "Focus, King. Just a few more minutes of video. This is the last school."

"Right." I turned back to the laptop on the conference table. The director and his team had scouted out Texas and narrowed it down to three high schools to shoot my next movie. All I had to do was pick one.

"We've heard from the girls—so how about a guy's reaction? Let's see what the guys in auto shop class think." The polished reporter with a perfect smile crouched down next to a car with the lower half of a guy's oil stained, coverall-clad body sticking out from underneath. "Excuse me, what are your thoughts on the news?"

The reporter stuck the microphone under the car, picking up an exasperated sigh before the student rolled out from under the car and sat up.

"Ma'am, I'm sort of busy here, so…"

"Oh! You're a girl." The reporter blinked a few times.

I wasn't talking about some woo-woo sixth sense, ESP, clairvoyance deal. I wasn't even sure what the "or else" was. But there was this gut feeling that if I didn't do this thing, I may miss out on something important. Something I may never get the chance at again.

"A girl? Ha! That's debatable!" Some guy yelled from off camera.

The girl shrugged one casual shoulder but her hands went white-knuckled around the wrench she held.

"So, I guess you're excited about the news." The reporter shifted the microphone back in front of the girl.

"What news?" The girl brushed a loose curl of chestnut hair from her cheek, leaving a streak of grease behind. "If you're about to tell me the school board is finally going to fund more vocational training in schools, then yes. Very excited."

"Oh, no. I was referring to the news about Kingsly Grant." Ms. Reed flashed the girl a wide smile.

"Who's Kingsly Grant?"

"Did she just say, 'Who's Kingsly Grant?'?" my agent asked, totally stupefied that there was one teenage girl on the planet who didn't know me.

The reporter looked as surprised as Frank.

"Uh… He's the hottest young actor in Hollywood right now." The reporter's smile had gone stiff and she darted her gaze around probably trying to find someone else who'd give her the response she was looking for.

"Oh, right. I think my friend Lacey made me go see one of his movies," the girl said, not looking very excited about me or my movie.

The reporter frowned but plowed on. "Is it exciting to think he may choose your school to film his next movie?"

"Exciting?" She shrugged, her gaze shifting to the undercarriage of the car as if impatient to get back to work before moving back to the reporter. "Why? Pretty sure he puts his perfectly faded, over-priced designer jeans on the same as everyone else."

"She's right about that," I said, grinning.

Some guy moved into the camera shot.

"I told you. She's not a real girl. Move aside, *Bernard.*" The dude pushed the flat wheeled dolly the girl sat on out of the camera range with his foot. I caught her eye roll just as she wheeled from sight. "We're stoked about King coming to our school. He's awesome. A movie star right here at Jackson? That's awesome."

I'd only had this spark of intuition happen two other times in my life. Sure, I was only eighteen, but those two times when I acted on my intuition were life-changing. In the best way. I guess what I'm saying is I was ninety-nine percent sure I was going to act on this hunch.

"Okay, I've seen enough." I hit the escape key to exit the video and closed the laptop. "How much time do I have to decide? I'm on vacation for the next four weeks. Can I let you know when I get back?"

"About that... The studio wants you to do another PR tour. They're aiming for a box office surge over spring break. Are you sure you can't postpone your vacation? Or cut it short to squeeze in some appearances?"

"I did the two-month press junket. Twenty cities, four countries, smiled my way through every interview and didn't turn a single one down." I shoved a hand through my hair and let out a breath. "It was grueling, Frank, you know that. I need this time off."

"Okay. I hear you." Frank pushed some paperwork across the desk. "Here's the revised script for you to read. Also, Alison is still not pleased you won't let her go on vacation with you."

"Ha! I bet." Alison was my personal trainer. She was the sweetest person—until she got in the gym. Then she turned into Hollywood's version of a drill sergeant. She was hard-core about working out, which was why I was ripped. But I wasn't planning on working out on vacation. "Please tell me she didn't give you a workout schedule to give me."

"Sorry, kid." Frank grinned as he pushed across the newest high-tech workout watch with a note. "She's pre-loaded four weeks of workouts."

"Let me guess... Alison will be tracking my workouts."

I told you she was hard-core. Which was why I paid her. She

was the best. Only, I had a plan for something different for the next few weeks. But I'd figure out a work-around for the app.

"You know it." Frank pushed across another sheet of paper. "Here's your meal plan from Stu."

My nutritionist. Right. I wouldn't need that either, but I took it anyway.

"You know," I looked around the table at my team with a grin. "It's almost like you're all going to be right there with me on my vacation. I'm feeling all warm and fuzzy inside."

"Ha! Well, we love you, kid," Donna said.

I knew they did. I wasn't just a paycheck to them. I mean, I was that too. Big ones. But my parents made sure the people on my team were good people. Professionals who cared more than just about the bottom line. They did love me and I loved them right back.

Which was why I felt a little guilty about my plans.

"I still need the details of where you'll be," Frank said, ready with a pen to jot it down.

"Not this time. Seriously, I'll be off the grid for four weeks." I needed this time away. For a few reasons. The least of which was that it would be my first vacation in over three years.

"What if something happens?" Frank frowned. "Or what if Ridley calls with an offer? You killed it at the audition."

"If it's an actual emergency, you can reach me through my parents. Anything else can wait." I narrowed my gaze at my agent. "We both know they're still auditioning for that role."

"It was worth a try," Frank said. "I don't like the idea of not being able to get a hold of you. We haven't been out of communication since the day I signed you."

"I know." Which was why I needed this. I needed time to *not* be Kingsly Grant. Don't get me wrong. I loved my life. I worked hard to get where I was and I loved it. But still…these next four weeks were going to be important. I wasn't even sure exactly why yet. Let's just say, I had a gut feeling.

WHO WOULDN'T WANT TO BE ME?

Bernadette "Bernie" Jewell

Who wouldn't want to be me right now? My dad was gone (for four months). My mom was gone (forever). I had two grandmas who professed to love me, yet one kept betting against me (literally), and the other didn't get me (at all).

It was only seven in the morning and I'd already killed the microwave which involved a small fire and our kitchen extinguisher (luckily close by).

Let me just say, it's easier to kill a microwave than I thought. Not that I'd thought about it much, but still...easy. I was running late for school (not normal) so I was rushing and managed to fry the microwave trying to heat up water for instant oatmeal when I forgot about the metallic rim of paint on my #girlmechanic mug. Hey, I was tired, okay? And who puts metallic paint on mugs anyway?

So now I was on breakfast attempt #2: heating leftover pizza up in a cast iron pan as I negotiated with my grandma (the betting one).

"Please, Gigi," I begged into my phone tucked between my

ear and shoulder while I flipped the pizza around with a fork. "Please come. It's your turn."

"It is, but your grandma Lolli asked to trade."

"Ugh. You know why, don't you?"

"I do." I was pretty sure I heard my grandma snicker.

"Why would you encourage her?" I loved both my grandmothers, but like I said, Lolli just didn't get me.

"Sweetie, she loves you. And...she misses your mama. So be patient with her, Bernie. And if it helps, between you and Lolli, my money's on you."

To be clear, my grandma Gigi was not speaking metaphorically. I sighed. "How much did you bet this time?"

"Only twenty bucks," she said, pausing a few seconds before adding, "Times four."

"*Are you kidding?*" I grabbed the handle of the pan only to pull my hand away quickly. "*Ouch!* Dang it, that hurts."

"What hurts?" Gigi asked.

"Nothing." I shut the burner off and shuffled over to the sink, sticking my burned hand under a stream of cool water with a sigh. The water ran over my palm, easing the pain down to a dull throb.

"Did you burn yourself again? I swear, Bernie, you're safer handling a welding torch in the garage than attempting anything in the kitchen."

This was true.

"I'm fine. It's barely pink," I said. Shutting off the water, I gently patted my palm dry with a paper towel. It was definitely tender. And an angry pink shade. Good thing it was my left hand.

"Is it blistering?"

"No. Back to the betting... *All* my brothers are betting against me?" I narrowed my eyes, already thinking about how I would get back at them. It would be harder since none of them lived at home anymore, but not impossible. Where there's a will there's a way.

"Well, they're brothers, so what did you expect?" Gigi said, definite laughter in her voice. Yes, she encouraged them too, dang it. "Fair warning...that's not the only bet we've got going on you."

"What else? Obviously, there's still the boyfriend bet." They'd placed bets last year on when I'd have a boyfriend. I wasn't anti-boyfriend. Between four older brothers and all of their friends, I'd grown up around a lot of boys. I'd tagged along behind my brothers and been treated like one of the guys when they were short a player for whatever pickup game they were playing.

It will not come as a surprise that I wasn't the girliest of girls. Most guys didn't even notice that I was a girl. And I had no idea how to attract a guy. Not that I was trying. In other words, no one was winning the boyfriend bet anytime soon.

My dad said when the right guy came along, he'd think I was beautiful no matter what I look like. He didn't mean that as an insult. He's a typical dad who thinks his daughter is beautiful. Of course, he also thought I looked like my mom—which I totally didn't see. I'd guess what he really meant was he was perfectly fine with not having to deal with guys dating his only daughter.

"Yes, the boyfriend bet. There's also money riding on when you're going to punch Todd Black in the face and when you'll give in and let Lacey give you a makeover."

"Well, never, never and never." I slid my backpack on one shoulder, grabbed the slice of pizza from the pan (very careful-ly!), my keys off the counter and left the house through the side kitchen door, locking it behind me. "I hope you bet wisely, Gigi."

"Eh. Maybe," she said. "How was your dad this morning?"

"Other than the fact that he tried to sneak out before I could say goodbye, fine." I sucked in a breath over our four-a.m. hug, opened my car door and tossed my backpack onto the passenger seat before sliding behind the steering wheel. My dad had a serious thing about goodbyes. "Luckily, I'm onto his tricks and I set my alarm an hour earlier than he said."

"Good for you. Hang in there, Bernie. The four months will fly by," Gigi said. "I'm only a phone call away."

"Ha! Says the grandma ignoring her only granddaughter's S.O.S. on the phone right now." I took a bite of pizza as I turned my key in the ignition, wincing when the engine didn't fire up right away. I knew my car was getting close to needing a new battery, but I'd been hoping it would last until my next paycheck. I tried again, feeding it more gas until it finally caught.

"I'm not ignoring you. Sometimes, you've got to live through an experience in order to learn life's greatest lessons."

"Bye, Gigi. If you aren't going to save me, I've got to get to school."

"Your grandma Lolli and I both love you. Never forget that. Now go set the world on fire."

That one I figured she meant metaphorically, but honestly, with my grandma Gigi, sometimes you just never knew.

* * *

Twenty minutes later as I sat in first period waiting for class to start, I was wishing I could set Todd Black's pants on fire. The bet on when I'd punch him in the face was in definite peril.

"Nice shirt, Bernard. Pretty sure I saw it in the boy's department at Target." He smirked his smirky face at me while his guy posse snickered around him. "Or are you wearing your brothers' hand-me-downs again?"

Like I usually did, I ignored him. I'd learned the hard way that feeding the beast usually backfired. And there was a high probability the T-shirt *was* one of my brothers' hand-me-downs.

"Who's entering the Texas State Auto Tech Competition this year?" Todd sat on top of his worktable, running his gaze around the room. "The deadline to enter is coming up and I want to get a good look at who's going to lose to me. Bernard, you have to sign up again. I could use the laugh."

I liked to think I was a nice person, but sometimes I tried to estimate how many Burger Barn Habanero burgers it would take—shoved into Todd's mouth—to get him to stop talking. Maybe two.

"Remember last year's competition, Bernard?" Todd asked loudly, making sure everyone in shop class could hear. "Man, it's a great memory."

Three. Definitely three.

"Hahaha. I still laugh thinking about how you thought you could compete against boys." He made one of those whistling noises that ended in a boom while his friends laughed and snickered. "You crashed and burned. Because girls suck as mechanics."

Four. I could totally shove four habanero burgers into his sexist pie-hole. Heavy on the habaneros until his face turned red and smoke came out his ears.

It was hard to swallow my failure at last year's competition and attempt to turn it into a positive with Todd's near-weekly reminders. It still stung. Enough that there was no way I was going to put myself through that again.

"Quiet down, people," Mr. Miles said, clumping through the doorway just as the late bell rang. "A couple things before you get started working today. First, we've got a new student joining us. This is Grant Stutterfield. I hope everyone will make him feel welcome at Jackson."

The new guy stood next to Mr. Miles. He wore sharply-ironed khaki pants short enough to see a couple inches of white athletic socks, a baggy hoodie with the words "cool kid" emblazoned across his chest, and a thick pair of black framed nerd glasses. Curls of blond hair peeked out from under a brand-new Jackson High ball cap.

"I'm sorry, I don't think I caught that last name... Did you say St-St-Stutterfield?" Todd asked, drawing laughs from his friends.

Five. Five burgers to shut Todd up.

"That's enough, Todd." Mr. Miles shot him a glance before grabbing his clipboard from his desk. "I'll need someone who can help get Grant up to speed. Todd, how about you?"

"I'd like to help, but I'm signing up for the state competition again, sir, and I'll be studying hard. I plan to make it to the national competition this year."

What a bunch of baloney. First, there was no way Todd wanted to help. Todd was a bully and a jerk. I doubted he even knew the meaning of the word "help." Second, he wouldn't be studying hard. Todd was a good mechanic, but he was cocky about it. Too cocky to study and work at getting better.

Mr. Miles nodded and looked back at the list, but I knew how this was going to go. The new guy was going to be forced to stand up there in the spotlight while everyone in class rejected him. Because Todd set the tone in class and most of the guys followed. It wasn't that all the boys in class were mean. Some were nice, but going against Todd was like painting a bullseye on your back. Speaking as Todd's number one target, I totally understood.

No point in putting the new guy through that.

"I'll do it," I said. Ignoring Todd's snort, I sent a nod to the new student. I expected to see his shoulders sag in relief, but instead he rolled his shoulders back and cocked his head. Dang. If he was just another Todd, thinking girls didn't belong in shop class, then I'd let him fend for himself.

The new guy hit me with his nerd-gaze. Something about

his brown eyes and the crooked smile on his lips turned my stomach into a taffy-pulling machine. Uh…whoa, what?

"Awesome. Grant, go ahead and take the empty seat at the back table." The new guy spared Todd one glance on his way past and settled on the stool next to me. "Pass your homework forward and then get to work finishing the electrical system lab."

I pulled out my paper on the comparison of disc and drum brakes and handed it to Gary at the next table who passed the stack in his hands on up until it landed on Mr. Miles's desk.

"Thanks. I really appreciate this," the new guy said. "So…I'm Grant and you are…?"

"Bernie Jewell."

"Bernie? Is it short for something?" Grant asked.

"Bernadette," I said. My parents had gone with all "B" names for my brothers. Brent, Brodie, Benjamin, and Brice. When they finally got to choose a girl's name, Bernadette was the only one they agreed on.

"Like the song by the Four Tops?" Grant asked.

I gave him the side-eye because no one in our generation knew that. Okay, except maybe Grady—but he was big into music. I tipped my head across the table. "That's Trig."

"Yo," Trig said without looking up from the pencil drawing he was doing in his notebook. Trig was big into comic books and only took shop so he could keep his car running.

"So… A girl in auto shop," Grant said.

"Uh huh. It's shocking, right?" I narrowed my gaze at the new guy. "Just like giving women the right to vote."

"Oh, hey. I didn't mean it that way." He pushed his glasses up with one finger. "I meant like it's cool."

"Whatever." Yes, I was a tad defensive, but, honestly, having to deal with kids like Todd did that to a girl. So, I'd give the new guy the benefit of the doubt—for now. I pulled out my shop class binder, pressed the tab to open the rings, and handed him over my notes. "Here you go. I'll need them back. Mr. Miles is pretty good about sticking to the syllabus, so the notes should be easy to follow."

"Can I...um...get your number? In case I have a question when I'm going through them." His brown eyes blinked innocently behind his glasses but I hesitated. I didn't like giving my number out to just anyone.

"Maybe Trig can—"

"Bern, it's not like he's going to call you for a date. Just give him your digits, yo."

Valid point. And that totally was not a swoosh of disappointment in my stomach at the thought. Nope. It was probably stress. I'd been thrown off the minute I saw my dad's note about Grandma Lolli arriving today taped to the fridge. Between that, setting the microwave on fire, and Todd bringing up last year again… Yeah, definitely stress.

"Okay." I leaned forward and wrote my cell number on the top page. "Feel free to text or call, you know, if you have a question."

Leaning into his space, I caught the scent of fresh soap and dryer sheets, which was very different from the normal high school shop odors of grease, oil, and too much Axe cologne. He smelled...nice. And what the heck was my problem? Since when did I notice how a guy smelled?

"Why don't I show you our car?" I jerked myself away and stood abruptly, moving toward the back of the huge room with three wide open garage doors. "All the shop classes are divided into three teams with each team working on one car. Our table is team two. The '79 Supra is ours."

"Sweet." Grant followed along next to me until we stood in front of the car's open hood gazing at the exposed transmission. "Or not. It's sort of a mess, isn't it?"

"Pretty much." I grinned down into the car. "That's what makes it so much fun."

Grant laughed next to me. "You like a challenge?"

"I like solving puzzles. Figuring out why a car isn't running has so many possibilities." I shrugged. "It's like being a detective."

He smiled at me and even though I tried not to notice—it was a great smile. I tore my gaze from him and back to the engine in front of me.

"You should know that Mr. Miles takes safety seriously. Everyone has to wear coveralls and goggles to work. Oh, and put tools away when you're done. It's another pet peeve of his. He's cool if students want to come work on the cars during lunch."

"Great. I'll need the extra time to get up to speed," Grant said. "Do you want to have lunch here today and work?"

"What?" I whipped my head around to look up at him. "Me? Oh, um… Sorry, no. I can't today."

"Okay. Sure." He grinned and shrugged. "But if you change your mind, you'll know where to find me."

Obviously, he was just asking me to eat lunch with him so I could help him. Not for any other reason. I wasn't trying to be mean, but between my dad leaving on deployment and my Grandma Lolli arriving, today wasn't a great day and I was looking forward to talking with my best friend Lacey at lunch.

"Why don't we go through the electronics? The coveralls are over on the hooks." I glanced from his loafers up his pressed khaki pants to his "cool kid" hoodie and up, realizing how very tall he was. At five foot eight inches, I was a tall girl myself but he had a half a foot on me. "You probably need to ask Mr. Miles for an extra-tall coverall."

"Hey, cool kid!" Todd called from where he stood at the hood of his team's car. "Come over and check this out!"

Grant looked over and then back at me. "Why did he call me cool kid?"

"Your shirt?" I tipped my head toward his chest before

glancing over at Todd with a shake of my head. "I would advise you not to go look, but that's me."

"Whoa, they have a Dodge Viper," Grant said, his gaze moving between the Viper and the Supra and back to the Viper again. "I need to go look."

"Then you should. You'll want to borrow these," I said, handing him a set of work goggles. Vaya con Dios, cute naive nerd guy.

2

"COOL KID" SQUARED

Grant

I strapped the goggles on, adjusting them over my glasses while Bernie looked up at me with the most gorgeous pair of hazel eyes I'd ever seen. I couldn't decide if it was her long dark eyelashes that made her eyes so striking. Or the way she looked at me almost challenging me to like her. Or not like her. Like she could care less what I thought about her.

Not a look I was used to at all. And I loved it. Although the defensive way she notched her chin up made me think she wasn't as tough as she seemed. Which reeled me in even more. It was right then that I realized I'd been standing staring at her like, well, like an awkward nerd. So, achievement unlocked.

I'd always played the cool kid on TV. And as I got older, the super cool good guy on the big screen. So yes, I thought my "cool kid" hoodie was ironic and I was having fun playing the nerd. Probably too much fun and overplaying a little. But most people saw what they expected to see.

The number one thing people recognized Kingsly Grant for was his eyes. I mean, my eyes. My eyes were a very light blue.

...ik Chris Pine blue. Or old school Hollywood Paul Newman blue. But Grant Stutterfield had brown eyes. My brown contacts would stop the majority of people from even thinking I reminded them of someone famous. The human brain was a wonderful thing.

It was when those hazel eyes narrowed that I realized I was *still* staring at Bernie. *Pull it together.* I quickly jerked my gaze from hers, turned away and walked over to check out the Viper.

Todd stood ready to draw me in until we both stood in front of the car's open hood.

"Well, what do you think?" He nodded down to the bright shiny engine.

"Nice. Very nice." And very different from my team's car. "How did your team end up with a Viper while the other team has a Supra?"

"My dad donated this one." Todd crossed his arms over his puffed out chest. "So our team has a *real* car to work on."

"Is that a 427 engine?" I leaned down to get a closer look.

"Sure is. A 7 liter 427 with 659 horse power." Todd slapped my back. "Have you seen anything this sweet before?"

I actually had. I'd been allowed to visit one of the shooting locations for the most recent Fast & Furious movies. Talk about sweet cars. Not to mention all the Hollywood actors I knew with fancy high-end cars. But a cool car was still a cool car.

"It's very nice."

"Wait until you hear her." Todd gave a thumb's up over the hood and then pointed back into the engine. "See that? Get a look back behind the alternator."

I leaned further in, craning my neck to see. "No, I—"

"Hang on. Fire her up, Mark!"

The engine roared to life and before I could move back, a stream of oil spurted out, hitting me directly in the face. I jumped back, oil dripping from my face, down my neck, and landing in splotches on my hoodie.

The Viper shut off, letting me hear the hooting and laughing around me. Wiping the coating of oil from the goggles, I glanced at Todd.

"Man, sorry about that." Todd stood grinning wide, not looking sorry at all. "Guess we need to check some hoses."

"Looks like it," I said, prompting another round of laughter from around the car. Todd's, of course, the loudest. Well, I wanted research; I was getting it in spades on my first day already.

I walked back over to where Bernie stood leaning over the Supra working.

"Well, that was fun." I pulled the goggles off. "Thanks for these, by the way."

"To be fair, I tried to stop you." She handed me a shop rag.

"Not very hard," I said, running a rag over my face and neck before wiping off the goggles.

She shrugged. "It's like my grandma Gigi says, 'Sometimes, you've got to live through an experience in order to learn life's greatest lessons.'"

"What did I learn just now?"

"Whoa, no. That's not how it works. You tell me—what did you learn?"

"That my 'cool kid' hoodie isn't cool."

"That may be a moot point unless you get that oil out soon." Her gaze flicked down to my sweat shirt and back up to my face. "That's it? That's all you learned?"

"No. Mostly I learned that Todd is a jerk."

"See? So it wasn't a wasted experience. There's some dish soap over by the sink that's pretty good with grease if you want to try to save your shirt." Her lips tilted up into a sweet smile. "I definitely think the cool kid hoodie should live to see another day. It'll be our inside joke reminding us how uncool Todd is."

"Has anyone ever told you that you've got a twisted mind?" I grinned at her.

"No."

"How did Todd manage that neat trick anyway?" I asked. "I feel like Judd Nelson in Beverly Hills Cop falling for the banana in the tailpipe."

"A pinprick in the oil pump supply line. You're not the first guy to fall for it." She threw me a sympathetic glance. "Seriously though, you'll need to wash your shirt now or it'll stain."

"It's okay." I wanted to be cemented into everyone's head as a "nerd" before I took off my baggy sweatshirt. Millions of people —a majority of them teenage girls—admired my physique. Not that nerds didn't work out, but I didn't want to take a chance of blowing my cover on the first day. Looking into Bernie's eyes— eyes so clear and full of honesty they took my breath away. No flirtation, or calculation, or breathless adoration. I wanted these four weeks more than I'd wanted anything in a long time. "I've got another one just like it."

"Ah, cool kid squared. Then let's get to work." Bernie flipped the Toyota car manual to the electrical system section and laid it on the rim of the open engine. "Electrical system. Prepare to be shocked."

"Ha! Very funny."

The only thing shocking was how quickly time flew by. Before I knew it, the bell sounded throughout the halls, class ended, Bernie slipped out before I could say goodbye, and it was time for me to join the scrum out in the hallways.

The noise level and mass of bodies pressing around me felt a lot like getting mobbed by screaming fans. Only these kids wanted nothing to do with me. They yelled and pushed their way past to get to friends or maybe their next class. Even as tall as I was, I got bumped around and pushed aside. I finally arrived at my locker and tried to slide in to open it.

"Dude, watch it!" the guy one locker over warned.

"Hey, sorry." Like I could help it that my 6'2 frame didn't fit into the twelve inch space in front of my locker.

"You're the new guy, right?" Some other guy had leaned up against the locker on my other side where he stood dragging his gaze over me before he slapped me on the back. "Welcome to Jackson. The robotics club meets after school on Thursdays."

"Um, thanks. Are you in the club?"

"Do I look like a loser? No, but I figured it was right up your alley." He high-fived his friend over his dunk on me and left.

See? This was the stuff I'd missed out on by growing up on a Hollywood set.

By the time I found my next class I was late. So much for sliding in surreptitiously. As soon as I stepped inside the classroom, I was in the spotlight.

"You must be our new student. Welcome, Mr. Stutterfield." The teacher held a textbook out to me with a smile. "I'm Miss Rose. Go ahead and take any empty seat."

Accepting the book, I pushed up my glasses and aimed toward the first available desk only to be waved off with a frown and a head shake. The same happened to the next two seats.

"Pssst, new guy," a voice hissed.

I ran my gaze around to find the voice and found two girls motioning me over to the empty desk in front of them. I nodded and made my way over, aware of the snickers and whispers circling the room.

"Thank you, Rowena. If you could help with the note, too…" Miss Rose said, clearing her throat to quiet the class down. "We're better than that here at Jackson, aren't we, people?"

I felt a tug on the back of my shirt and then the girl, Rowena, passed me the small post-it note from my back.

I'M NOT
FRIENDLY.
I JUST LIKE
TO SMILE
AFTER I FART.

Oh, nice. Guess some kids at Jackson High *weren't* better than that. On the plus side, this was awesome research. I slid the note inside my textbook to save.

"Okay, class. Let's discuss last night's reading assignment. Who can tell me what the 'hero's journey' is?" Miss Rose looked around the room. "Chad, what is the hero's journey?"

"Uh… well, that's when Luke saved Princess Leia and blew up the death star, right?" Chad slouched further down in his seat.

"Star Wars is an example of the hero's journey, yes. But I was looking for a more substantive answer." Miss Rose arched an eyebrow at him. "From our reading."

The teacher's gaze shifted to the girls behind me.

"Hang on, girls. I'm hoping to hear from some of our quieter voices. Did anyone other than Rowena and Shani do the reading assignment? Brad, Ashely, anyone? Gwen, how about you?"

"The hero's journey?" Gwen asked, twirling a strand of long blond hair. "That's like when a hero goes on a long trip. Not usually by plane, though. And he does hero stuff, you know, like fighting and stuff. Sometimes he dates Sandra Bullock."

Laughter broke out around the room.

"So that's a 'no' on the homework." Miss Rose shook her head. "No one else?"

I slowly raised my hand. Why the heck not? I was posing as a nerd, right?

"Grant, give it a shot."

"The hero's journey is a classic plot structure in fiction made popular by Joseph Campbell. The journey can be divided up into seventeen steps or three stages: the call to adventure and departure of the ordinary world, initiation into unknown territory, and the return in triumph. Sometimes that ends with dating Sandra Bullock. But sometimes Sandra Bullock is the hero who returns in triumph."

"That is correct, Mr. Stutterfield. Send a thank you note to your last English teacher for me." She smiled at me before turning to the girl Gwen. "Grant makes a good point to remember. Females take the hero's journey too. Scout, Katniss, Amari, and even in non-fiction, such as Malala Yousafzai or author bell hooks."

Some guy in the back coughed out "nerd alert" and "dork" while half the kids in class snickered.

"That's enough, Chad. Back to the hero's journey…Campbell stated that…" Miss Rose lectured until the end-of-class bell sounded, wrapping up by calling out, "Fair warning! I'm putting pop quizzes back on the menu, so start doing your homework, people. Class dismissed."

I spun around to the girls behind me. "Thanks for the seat."

"Sadly, it means you're officially a nerd. I'm Rowena; you can call me Ro." She tilted her head to the girl next to her. "This is Shani."

"Ha! Pretty sure that answer he gave made his nerd status official." Shani smiled at me. "Where did you transfer from?"

"Oh, uh, California."

"Nice," Shani said. "You're welcome to join us for lunch in the cafeteria."

"Thanks. I just might." I definitely needed to experience the cafeteria. Wasn't that the place to see the hierarchy of cliques on full display? And if I didn't see Bernie in there, at least I had my Funyuns, Little Debbie snack cakes, and Skittles to look forward to.

3

DIABOLICALLY DELICIOUS

Bernie

A few days later.

The beautiful sweet scent of homemade blueberry pancakes hit my consciousness just as I slapped my alarm off. Oh man, my grandma Lolli was devious.

I rolled out of bed, threw on my favorite hand-me-down T-shirt (it was oversized, soft from years of washing, and the old school Pokémon logo still clearly visible) along with a pair of baggy camouflage cargo pants. Since I didn't carry a purse, the many pockets came in handy. I tamed my curly hair by dragging it back into a low ponytail and splashed cold water on my face. I would need to be alert and on my game to deal with Lolli and her delicious pancake bribe.

After shoving my books into my backpack, I sat to pull on socks and my well-worn oil-stained Timberland boots, took a deep breath and headed downstairs to the kitchen.

"Morning, Lolli." I dropped my backpack on a chair on my way to the fridge.

"Good morning." Lolli tossed me a bright smile from where

she stood at the stove. "I made your favorite blueberry pancakes."

"They smell great. You're going to spoil me while dad's away." I retrieved two glasses from the cupboard and poured milk into each. "Both of us usually eat cereal or frozen waffles for breakfast."

"I know." She laughed as she dished the pancakes onto plates, handing one to me. "That won't happen on my watch."

We settled at our small pine table and she let me get three whole bites down before she made her move.

"So... I ran into town yesterday and look what I picked up." She pushed a flier across the table at me. I didn't need to look. I knew exactly what it was. I shoved a big bite of pancake in my mouth so I had an excuse not to respond while I figured out how I was going to turn her down this year.

Two years ago, I'd resorted to tears—not full tears, since I wasn't that good, but I got them to well up in my eyes by thinking about when my old dog Herbert passed away. Yes, I felt guilty about resorting to tears, but I was only sixteen and desperate.

Last year, I claimed I hadn't recovered from the sprained ankle I'd gotten playing pick-up football with the neighborhood guys over winter break. It was sort-of the truth.

"The Miss Armadillo Pageant. This is your last year of eligibility."

"Lolli..."

"Sweetheart, it's tradition in our family." Here it was. Lolli was going for the big sale. "It started with your great grandma Fritzie being the first runner-up. Then of course I was crowned Miss Armadillo when I was sixteen. Then your mama won. She beat out those Martin triplets, and everyone knows Eunice Martin tried to bribe the judges with her pickle pie."

I froze with my fork half-way in the air. "Uh... Please tell me that isn't some weird euphemism for—"

"Goodness no! She won the blue ribbon at the Texas State Fair three years in a row with her pickle pie. Luckily it did *not* sway the judges and your mama was rightfully crowned."

"Yay."

"I simply don't understand why you won't enter, Bernie." Lolli frowned. "It's so much fun. You get to wear a pretty gown, show off your talent, and share camaraderie with other girls."

"Lolli, I'm not like you or mama. I don't do dresses and I don't have a talent." And other than my best friend Lacey, my ability to bond with other girls went down exponentially the more I tried. I didn't do gossip, care about fashion, or watch the latest reality TV dating show. Not many girls wanted to discuss cars, sports scores, or the need for vocational training.

"You do too have a talent. You make beautiful lamps."

"Thank you for the compliment, but I *weld* them." I'd begun making lamps out of old engine parts when I was learning to weld in order to work on cars. It turned out people liked them, so I began selling them to pay for car parts. "I can guarantee you the fire marshal would be a little upset if I fired up my welding torch on stage."

"You make a good point. What about your music? You play the accordion." She beamed at me as if she'd laid down a royal flush in one of our family night button poker games.

"I've only started teaching myself." And I only did it as a joke. I'd discovered Grandma Gigi's old accordion in the attic over the summer and thought she'd bust a gut if I played her a song with it.

"All you need is one song. I heard you play one yesterday."

"No. You heard me fumble through half a song." I took a drink of milk while I counted to ten. Lolli was sweet and I appreciated that she and Gigi took turns to come stay with me when Dad's reserve unit deployed. But this pageant stuff was frustrating. "Lolli, I don't have a talent. If the Beach Boys heard how badly I'm butchering 'Kokomo,' they'd have me arrested."

"I thought it sounded wonderful," Lolli said with a sniff.

Sure she did. Because grandmas always thought their grandkids were amazing. Plus, she was clinging to this pageant dream like it would complete her life. Like between the three generations I would be the final win in her Miss Armadillo Triple Crown. Lolli needed more hobbies for sure.

"I've gotta go." I cleared my dishes to the sink, grabbed up my backpack, wrapped two pancakes to go in a napkin and made for the door. "Have a great day."

"What about the Miss Armadillo Pageant?" Lolli asked.

I had my foot on the first step outside and escape seconds away, but I paused in an attempt to end this madness.

"I love you very much." I smiled at her, hoping she'd take this well. "But I'd rather wrestle a rabid armadillo in a tank filled with pudding before I entered the Miss Armadillo Pageant."

"So, you won't even consider it?" She raised one eyebrow. Never a good sign. Lolli could be stubborn as a bull when she got something in her mind. "This is your last chance. I hate the idea of you passing it by. It's so important."

"Lolli, I'm so far from the pageant type of girl, it's silly."

"How do you know? You've never been in one."

"Wow, look at the time. I don't want to be late for school!" I let the screen door flutter shut behind me and hustled to my car before she could reformulate another line of attack.

For a girl who didn't do drama, my life was starting to feel a little tense. Part of the problem was that I usually talked this kind of stuff over with Lacey. Between Dad leaving for deployment, Lolli and the pageant, the new guy Grant, Todd being even jerkier than usual, and needing more hours at work so I could replace my car battery (Lolli had insisted on replacing the microwave)…things felt like they were piling up.

But Lacey had a lot going on too, what with the talent showcase at school. I knew she was on the verge of freaking out, so I wouldn't add to her stress. I felt like an overheating engine with pressure building and the temperature gage spiking to the red zone.

After parking in my assigned spot at school, I grabbed my backpack and napkin-wrapped pancakes and walked in the front entrance only to run into Lacey, standing leaning against one of the poster-filled columns.

"Hey! I've been waiting for you." Lacey gave me her usual bright smile, only to have it fade. "What's wrong?"

"Nothing's wrong." She had more going on than I had, so I could hold off and talk to her after this weekend. The simple fact that my best friend could take one look at my face and know all was not right in my world made me feel better.

"Uh huh. First, I don't believe that." She arched an eyebrow at me. Yep. We may be total opposites, but she knew me. "Second, I'm so sorry I've been distracted by the whole talent showcase. But it's over this weekend and then you and I are having a talk where you will confess all. Deal?"

"Deal," I said.

"Third, do I smell Lolli's blueberry pancakes?" Lacey's gaze was glued to the pancake stash in my hand. "Please tell me you brought those to share with your best friend."

"You know I did." I handed her a pancake and took a bite of my own.

"I love you even more than I did thirty seconds ago. And thirty seconds ago I would have told you I couldn't love you more." Lacey took a bite and moaned in pleasure as she chewed. "Sweet, tart, and light as air. Your grandma's pancakes are the food of angels."

"I know," I said, taking another bite as we both walked down the hall to our first period class. Today was a "B" day and we both had Mrs. Marcou for Advanced Calculus.

"Oh, no! I just realized what's coming up." Lacey's gaze rose from her pancake over to me. "Is this part of Lolli's push for the pageant again?"

"Yep." I sighed. "As bribes go, they're diabolically delicious."

"They really are. If it helps, I volunteer to eat all the pancake bribes for you."

I laughed. "So noted."

* * *

At lunch time, I stopped by the front office to deliver my latest letter championing the need for continued funding for vocational training at the high school level. Principal Barstow hand-delivered my letters to each Board of Education meeting.

In my dreams, I hoped my letters would make an impression although they hadn't yet. That didn't stop me from trying though. Along with letters to the Board, I'd written letters to many non-profit and charity organizations for grants to keep Jackson's vocational education funded.

"Hi, Mrs. G," I said, handing my letter to the secretary. "Can you make sure Principal Barstow gets this?"

"Absolutely." She took the envelope and winked at me. Was she trying to boost my morale since she figured vocation funding was a lost cause? "I was just about to send a runner for you. Mrs. Loftus, the new counselor, wanted to talk with you."

Mrs. G handed me the blue counseling slip.

"What happened to Dr. Boyd?"

"Early retirement. I think Mrs. Loftus is free right now if you have time."

"Sure."

Her door was off to the left, down a short hallway. I knocked on her open door and she waved me in from her desk.

"Mrs. Loftus? I'm Bernie Jewell. Mrs. G said you wanted to see me."

"Yes! Please sit. I've been working my way through all of the student's records and noticed you records seem incomplete. Did you have your college advisory meeting with Dr. Boyd before he retired?"

"Yes, ma'am. I did." I nodded and perched on the edge of the chair in front of her desk.

"We try to encourage each student to select five universities to apply to and then include a few reach schools. I don't see your list in your file."

"I plan to go to technical school." She stared at me with a blank look so I added, "To become a certified mechanic. Although, I haven't decided between cars or diesel truck engines yet."

"A mechanic?" A wrinkle creased between her eyebrows. "But you've got excellent grades. You could study engineering or physics or even pre-med based on your SAT math score alone. Your verbal score is excellent also."

"But I enjoy working with my hands." I'd had this same conversation with Dr. Boyd.

"There are so many exciting opportunities for girls these days." She leaned forward, clasping her hands in front of her on the desk. "You can absolutely reach higher than trade school."

"I understand. May I ask you a question, Mrs. Loftus?"

"Oh, absolutely," she said, sending me a bright smile as she pushed a fancy folder emblazoned with *College: Your Ticket to the Stars* across her desk to me.

"Is that a photo of your daughter?" I nodded to a photograph on the file chest behind her.

"It is." The love on her face shone brightly. "That's Emma. Of course, right now she's fourteen going on twenty, so a handful, but we love her."

"Right? So when Emma starts to drive, just out of curiosity, do you want a smart mechanic working on her car—say her brake lines—or the dumbest high school graduate?"

Mrs. Loftus blinked at me once. Twice. And then she

reached across the desk and pulled the folder back, placing it off to the side.

"How about we schedule an appointment to see about trade school scholarships?" she asked.

"That would be great."

I had left the office and was on my way toward the cafeteria to eat lunch when I got a text from Grant.

Grant: *Hey, Bernie. I hate to tell you this, but I might have killed our engine. Again.*

Me: *DO NOT TOUCH ANYTHING. I'll be right there.*

This was not the first time he'd texted me this. Just like the other two times, I totally broke school rules and ran through the hallway to shop class.

4

I MIGHT HAVE KILLED OUR ENGINE

Bernie

There were only a couple other guys in the classroom, but the one I was concerned with had his hands too close to our engine.

"Hands in the air, Stutterfield," I called from the doorway.

Grant lifted his hands away and turned to face me wearing a rueful grin.

"I'm sorry." He raised his goggles to rest on his forehead. "I was just trying to get caught up."

"If you could tell me what happened with the fewest number of words—that would help." I wasn't trying to be rude, but the loss in last year's state competition had been a dent to my confidence. And Todd's regular reminders and insults only made it harder. With each passing day of this school year, my determination to win the class team competition grew. "I'm sorry. That came out too harshly. It's just I really want our team to win this year."

"No apology necessary. Having met Todd, I get it."

I glanced over at the engine and could immediately guess what happened. "You dropped something down a cylinder."

"How did you—yes." He puffed out a breath. "I took off the intake manifold and I accidentally dropped a bolt in."

"Okay." I nodded. "This is not a problem. It would have been a problem if you hadn't noticed and we'd turned the engine on. *That* would have killed our engine."

"Good. So how do we get it out?"

"We'll have to take the engine apart," I said. Not a job I wanted to tackle.

"Apart?" Grant ran a hand through his blond hair and released a long whistle. "Man, I'm sorry. That's a big job."

"Or...if it's our lucky day—we won't." I walked to our toolbox and pulled out a flashlight and the trusty magnet I had glued onto the end of a flexible rod.

"You're going to fish for it?"

"That's the plan." I leaned over the engine, so I could look straight down into the cylinder, holding the flashlight aimed in one hand and my magnet in the other.

"I'll hold the flashlight," Grant said, taking it from me. He bent over the engine next to me, our bodies pressed close together as he aimed the light downward from just over my shoulder. "How's that?"

How's that? Distracting.

"Mmm hmm." I'd been working with Grant for a week now, but never *this* close. I was plastered up against his tall body and his deep brown eyes and his one-dimpled smile and that dryer sheet and fresh breeze scent and I almost forgot what we were doing. Almost. Flicking my gaze at him and away, I held the tool ready as I peered down to look. "Um, can you narrow the beam?"

"Sure. Has anyone told you that you have very pretty eyes?" he said, adjusting the light.

My hands froze. Because no one—well, no guy—had ever told me that. No guy who wasn't related to me had ever given me a compliment about my looks. Ever. So obviously, I had no idea how to react. "Yeah, well, has anyone told you that you smell good?"

"What?" Grant laughed.

"Nothing. I mean, I don't know. Whatever." I jerked my gaze back down to the emergency at hand before I made an even bigger idiot of myself.

"Bernie, look at me," he said, his deep voice vibrated through me all the way down to my toes.

"I'm kind of busy here," I said, having a very hard time keeping my hands steady, thanks to Grant and his pretty eyes comment. Geez, what was his problem?

"Bernadette, please look at me."

"Fine." I huffed out a breath and lifted my head to look. Our faces were a foot apart. "What?"

"I have no idea what's wrong with the guys around here, but that wasn't me being sarcastic. I was being totally sincere." His lips tilted up at the corners the smallest bit. "The brown in your eyes is rich and warm but up close you've got hidden facets of emerald green streaking through shining like jewels in the sun."

"Hazel," I whispered. "They're just hazel."

"They're not *just* hazel. They're beautiful," he repeated, his own eyes warm and friendly. "Do you really think I smell good?"

"Oh, man. I'll pay you five dollars to pretend I never said that." Fire spread through my cheeks so hot that Grant could probably get a sunburn if he stood too close. Like he was.

"I don't think so. I'm keeping that compliment." He grinned. "But I'll shut up now so you can save us from my mistake."

"O-okay. That'd be good." I leaned back over the engine, using all my concentration to refocus on the lost bolt. "Can you move the flashlight to the left?"

"Better?" His deep voice sounded in my ear and his clean laundry scent wrapped around me.

Focus, Bernie. Shut out the cute nerd and focus.

"A little more left. There. Hold it there." I peeked down inside the cylinder. "I don't see it, but hopefully it didn't roll too far."

Lowering the magnet, I eased up when it hit the bottom so it could gently bend into the curve hoping I didn't push the bolt further in. When I heard a slight click, I carefully raised the magnet back out, smiling wide to see the bolt along for the ride.

"Nice work," Grant said, lifting his hand in the air for a high five as we both straightened up.

"This wasn't my first lost bolt rodeo." I might not know what to do with a compliment, but I knew high fives. I'd been high-fiving guys since I was six. This was a language I could speak. So I slapped his hand in response.

Only he changed the rules. Before I could pull my hand away, his fingers intertwined with mine and held on. It was an extra connection I wasn't ready for. His hand was strong and warm around mine.

He held on until I looked into his eyes and we stood there, hands clasped, eye to eye, and it felt like the world around us came to a screeching halt.

"You doing anything this weekend?" he asked, finally letting go of my hand.

"W-why?"

"I thought maybe we could see each other."

"Me and you?" I cleared my throat. "I'm pretty busy this weekend. I've got the thing at school—"

"The showcase?" he asked.

"Yes, my friend and I are going. And I, um, promised my grandma I'd do stuff, and then I've got, you know, other stuff." I couldn't sound more ridiculous if I tried. But I was sure if I didn't end this convo soon—I'd manage it. "Glad we got this fixed. I've got to go...um..."

"Do stuff?" Grant asked, a gentle smile on his face.

"Right. Exactly right, and I'm late." I shoved the magnet and flashlight into his hands and left as fast as I could, ducking into the nearest girl's bathroom. I washed my hands at a sink while I pulled myself together. The thing was...no boy had asked me out before. Not like that. And I was totally, completely freaking out.

The sound of multiple toilets flushing and stall doors opening caught my attention.

"Jewell, what do I keep telling you?" Breanna Smith moved to the sink next to me and proceeded to do a seriously bad job at washing her hands while she stared at my reflection in the mirror with mocking eyes. "You don't belong in here. The boy's bathroom is down the hall."

"Yeah," one of Breanna's friends joined in. "Notice the lack of urinals in here, freak."

Right. I'd forgotten why I usually used the bathroom on the other side of school. I left without saying a word.

Well, that run-in with Breanna and her friends brought me clarity and the end to my freak out. To be honest, deep down I knew the whole time. Grant hadn't *really* asked me out. Not on a date. Whatever. I had stuff to go do.

5

JUST A REGULAR TEENAGER

Grant

"So, how do you like being a regular teenager?" Mom asked at breakfast Monday morning.

"Let me say, movie stereotypes of awkward nerds aren't that far off." I chased a marshmallow football around my cereal bowl with my spoon. "But even though I've had kids ignore me, push me around, slap signs on my back—yes, kids actually do that—snicker and laugh at me, and outright insult me…I love it. The first week went by too fast."

"I'm pretty sure that's because you ate yourself into a sugar coma on junk food." Mom laughed and shook her head as she watched me scarf down a second bowl of Cookies & Charms cereal in amused awe.

"Do you think I'm going overboard?" I paused with my spoon half-way to my mouth.

"I don't. You will never get me to admit this to Frank or anyone else on your team, but I love that you're doing this."

"Yeah?"

"I really do. You've been working since you were eight years old. You're the most dedicated, driven person I've ever known."

Mom moved over to the coffee machine and refilled her mug before turning back to me. "You know your dad and I support you in every way, but we've been worried too."

"Worried? You two have always been there with me. Been there *for* me." I tilted my head, not sure what she meant. "You interviewed and selected my team carefully."

"We absolutely did. What I mean is we worry that you've missed out on the little things. Normal things like a normal kid. So, this is fun for us too. Fun to watch you get to experience a normal life even if you had to go incognito to do it."

"Thanks, mom. Speaking of incognito—some guy at school recognized me at the showcase at school on Friday night."

"Oh, no." Mom's eyes went wide and she gripped the counter with her hands. "So that's it? You only had a week? I'm sorry, Grant."

"No, I think I'm okay. He didn't say anything when he recognized me."

"I'm amazed he did recognize you. I barely recognize you what with the contacts, extra pounds, and different hair style."

"Extra pounds?" I laughed and patted my stomach. "Okay, fine. Maybe a couple two, three or five pounds. But you know I'll take it off."

Of course, I'd probably have to do two-a-day workouts next month to make that happen. Nothing new when I was preparing for a role. Part of being Kingsly Grant was keeping my muscled physique. Which I did with the help of my trainer and my nutritionist. Plus when I set goals, I went all-in on achieving them. I'd been working out regularly and eating squeaky clean for four years now. That's a long time without junk food. Which was why I was ignoring the menu plan from Stu and giving in to the junk-food loving kid I'd kept in check for years.

"I do. I was kidding about the weight. To be honest, I've had fun baking for you again."

"I sure have missed your baking. You haven't baked since we hired Stu and he cut out sugar, flour, and anything remotely fun," I said. It wasn't Stu's fault. It was what I paid him for. Hollywood was competitive, and if an actor wanted to star in leading roles, they had to be willing to put in the hard work, on the set and off. "Anyway, I'm going to talk to the guy after school today."

"Probably a good idea," Mom said. "Don't forget—"

"What is that glorious smell?" I slid from my stool at the island, dropped my bowl into the dishwasher, and moved to the oven to peek in. "Monkey bread? You made monkey bread?"

"Oh, I almost forgot it!" Mom grabbed up a set of oven mitts, brushed me out of the way, and removed the cake pan. She flipped it out upside down on a plate and drizzled the whole beautiful thing with a cinnamon glaze. "There you go."

"Second breakfast!" I gave her a side arm hug while I spooned myself up a generous helping. She handed me a fork and I made quick work of it right where I stood. "Mmmm, Mom. Amazing. I haven't had this in years. Too bad Dad isn't here to share it."

"Ha! You don't look like you want to share." Mom shook her head. "I'll just make another when he comes in two weeks."

Dad was a lawyer out in L.A. so he hadn't been able to come to Texas with us for the full month. Since Mom now ran my charity foundation, she could do that from anywhere.

"I've got to get to school, although...I've never been tardy. That might be fun to experience." I side-eyed Mom to see her reaction and sure enough she gave me her eagle-eyed stare. "Or not. I'm out."

"Don't forget your lunch." She tipped her head over to the brown bag on the counter. "Made as requested. One PB&J sandwich, ranch potato chips, two Little Debbie dessert rolls and a bag of Skittles."

"Stu and Alison would have a heart attack if they knew what

I was eating." I couldn't stop my grin as I grabbed the lunch. Like I said, it was completely my choice that I'd been eating healthy and super-clean. But since I was taking a vacation from my top box-office selling movie star life, I wasn't going to let this opportunity slip by.

I wanted to slurp up bowls of sugary cereal and doughnuts for breakfast. Enjoy fast food with French fries for lunch, sit in the bleachers while I munched on popcorn and rainbow colored candies. Eat one of my mom's carb-loaded casseroles for dinner followed by a huge dish of caramel covered ice cream for dessert. Was it wrong to want a taste of what I'd been giving up the last four years? Ha. Taste… See what I did there?

This wasn't about regretting my life choices. Not at all. Every step on my path as an actor had been my choice. I didn't have pushy stage parents. In fact, my parents had sacrificed a lot to help support me and my dreams. Big sacrifices, like moving from Texas, where they both grew up, to L.A. when I starred in my first TV show at eight.

"Speaking of Alison, she texted me twice last week asking if you were okay." Mom raised one eyebrow at me. "She's worried."

"Well, shoot. I forgot about the workouts." I grabbed my backpack. "I don't want to worry her. I'll take care of it."

"Don't forget we need to sit down together one night this week to finish looking through the grant requests and decide on this year's charity donations."

"I'm not forgetting. I'm looking forward to that," I said. "Off to school. Hey, maybe I should go for the full high school experience and get detention."

"You could… But then your father and I would have to ground you to get the *full* experience."

"Ha!" Game, set, and match to my mom. She was onto my teasing ways and usually gave back as good as I gave her. "So no detention then."

. . .

I had another interesting day at school. Since it was "B" day, I didn't have shop with Bernie. And the few times I saw her throughout the day, she seemed to disappear as soon as she saw me. It happened in the cafeteria, and in the locker bay, and even when I tried to say hello when I saw her at her locker between fifth and sixth period. It almost felt like she was avoiding me, but why would she do that? Unless she was mad that I'd almost killed our engine for the third time.

By the time the last bell of the day rang, I had to stop thinking about Bernie and track down the guy Grady.

I walked out to the student parking lot with my head on a swivel looking for him.

"Grant!" Shani and Ro, my new friends from English class, stood behind a mini Cooper. "Do you need a ride? We're on our way to bowling practice, but we have time to drop you off somewhere."

"Actually, I'm looking for a guy named Grady. He played guitar in the showcase over the weekend. Any chance you know him?"

"Grady Burnett. Wasn't he great? He's a nice guy too."

"Do you know where I might find him?" I asked, casually.

"Wherever Lacey Trueheart is," Shani answered, making Ro giggle. "But seriously, he's on the lacrosse team."

"If you don't see him in the parking lot, he'll be at the lower practice field," Ro said, pointing off to the left behind the school.

"Great."

"Is it something we can help you with?" Shani asked.

"Thanks, but no. I just need to confirm something that came up in a conversation I had with him." If Grady Burnett recognized me like I thought he did, I needed to see if he'd keep my secret. If not, my vacation was over.

I looked around the lot while I walked to my car to store my backpack. After giving it a few minutes without seeing him, I followed Ro's directions down to the lacrosse field and found Grady. As soon as he saw me, his eyes went wide and he sprinted over to meet me.

"Grady, right?" I asked. We stood face to face, eying each other carefully.

"That's me." He peered closer at my face. "The question is... who are you?"

6

WHO ARE YOU?

Grant

The question is...who are you?

"I'm not sure how...but I think you already know," I said, raising my eyebrows at him and staring him in the eyes.

"Dude, this is cool." His gaze did an up-and-down over me. "Kingsly Grant."

"How *did* you know? I thought my disguise was good. Subtle, but good."

"It is. You're sort of rocking the bro Thor look." Grady grinned at me.

"Ha! Well, right now I'm Grant Stutterfield and I'm enjoying *not* being King for a few weeks." I glanced to the field where the rest of the team was preparing for practice. "You think other people will figure it out too?"

"Nah. Seriously, the dark contacts alone sort of do it. I only recognized you because I happen to have one of the few copies sold of the never-hit-wonder boy group, Nick & Pals."

"Get out." I burst out laughing. Sometime between the long-running TV show I grew up on and my first movie role, I was in a boy band for five minutes. "Hardly anyone even knows about that. Why would you have a copy? It was pretty bad."

"I agree, it was pretty bad. The lead singer—Nick—yeah, he was horrible. But the band's guitarist? That guy had talent. I watched a few of your videos over and over, trying to copy your style on stage when I was first learning to perform."

"I heard you in the showcase. You're good," I said. "You're a better guitar player than I ever was."

"Thanks." Grady nodded once. "So what are you doing at Jackson? Is this some PR stunt for *Seventeen Summers?*"

"No. I guess it's a combination of research and…a vacation."

"Research?" he asked.

"My next movie is set in high school—"

"Heard that." Grady shrugged. "The local news even showed up."

"Sorry. Or you're welcome. Whichever way you feel about it. I've been tutored almost my whole life, so I'm doing some research. I figured I needed to experience high school to portray it accurately." My gaze roamed over the scene in front of me from the players on the field, over to a group of cheerleaders practicing on the track, and up to the metal bleachers scattered with a handful of students. "The cliques, classes, clubs, sports— all of it."

"All of it, huh? Awesome." Grady wrapped an arm around my shoulders and led me toward the field. "You'll want to experience playing a team sport then. It so happens, we're short a goalie."

"What?" I laughed. "I have no idea how to play lacrosse, let alone goalie."

"Dude, you're like six foot and change. Even if all you do is stand in front of the goal, you'll block half the shots."

My watch sounded, reminding me I still had to deal with the workouts.

"Sorry, Grady, I can't help." I stopped walking and stared down at my watch. "I've got to deal with this."

"What is that?" He leaned in for a look. "Oh, man, is that one of those Garmin workout watches? Coach has one and it's lit. What do you mean you have to deal with it?"

"My trainer is a little obsessive and she's freaking out that I haven't been doing my workouts. I wasn't planning on working out on vacation, but…" I looked at Grady with a shrug. "Sorry—"

"Not so fast, Stutterfield. I believe we can help each other. You fill in for goalie—"

"I'm only here for three more weeks," I said.

"Perfect timing. That's all we need since that's how long our goalie's out. So, you fill in for our injured goalie and I'll handle your workouts."

"Seriously?"

"Watch and learn," he said, dragging me the rest of the way to the field and over to the coach. "Coach, I've got our new goalie while Rob's out with his broken leg."

"Whoa, what?" How rough was lacrosse? "You didn't tell me your goalie broke his—"

"Relax. He broke it trying to moonwalk on a treadmill." He turned back to the coach. "This is Grant Stutterfield. He just transferred from California and is a solid goalie."

"Coach, that's not—" I started to say, only Grady smacked his elbow into my stomach.

"I'm happy to see you. Welcome aboard, Grant." Coach nodded. "Go ahead and run the captain's warm ups, Grady."

"Yes, sir, coach." Grady pulled me with him into the center of the field. "Bring it in, guys."

He motioned to two guys who joined the line with him. "Grant, these are the other co-captains with me. Dax and TJ. Guys, this is Grant. Grant's our new goalie."

"Awesome," Dax said, holding up his fist for a fist bump which I answered.

"Grant...watch. Hand it over." Grady held his hand out to me, wiggling his fingers for it.

I handed it over.

"Okay, everyone, listen up. Before we run warm-ups, we're announcing a new fitness competition. You know how we run out of gas in the last ten minutes of every game? Right. That's going to stop." Grady held up the Garmin watch for all to see. "Team competition. Every player will take one turn at this new top secret workout program I found on line. All workouts will be judged on cardio, heart rate, max reps, and..."

Grady slid his gaze over to me.

"VO$_2$ max levels," I added. "It's mostly Hiit training."

"We'll go by jersey number starting with 1 and work up. That means you're up first, Dax." He handed the watch over to Dax who looked athletic.

"Cool." Dax stared down at the watch before latching it onto his wrist. "Not to brag, but I plan to set the bar high."

"What's the prize for winning?" some guy called from the back of the circle.

"Better fitness and more wins isn't enough for you?" Grady shook his head.

"The prize is a..." I glanced at Grady since I had no idea what guys in Texas considered a worthy prize.

"A fifty-dollar gift card to Burger Barn," Grady said to the enthusiasm of the whole team.

"Works for me," TJ said. "All right, let's get warmed up."

Everyone spread out as Grady turned to give me a wide smile.

"Done. Welcome to the team, Stutterfield."

I wasn't sure what I'd gotten myself into, but the idea of playing a team sport was pretty sweet.

"Since you're not dressed to workout, I'll have Rob coach

you on basic goalie skills. Tomorrow you can start full practice."
Grady turned toward the sidelines where the cheerleaders were
practicing and called into the bleachers. "Big Rob! Come down
here and help our new goalie!"

A dude taller and a lot wider than me grabbed up a pair of
crutches and hobbled onto the field.

After introductions were made, Grady jogged off and left me
under the tutelage of Rob. He spent a half hour going over the
basics of handling the goalie stick, covering the goal, and how to
clear the ball downfield. Next, he handed me his goalie mask
and pads to wear and he took some shots with me as goalie. It
turned out there was way more to stopping the ball than
standing in front of it.

When coach called an end to practice, Rob shook his head
and frowned at me. "How long have you played goalie?"

"How long have we been practicing?" I asked, dragging the
mask from my face.

"You've never played goalie?" Rob nodded, looking relieved.
"That explains it then. Okay, not a big deal. We can work
together during practice and you'll pick it up in no time."

I didn't bother to tell him I'd never played lacrosse. He'd
probably figure that out at tomorrow's practice.

Grady walked over and slapped my back. "How'd it go?"

"If you, Dax and TJ play stellar offense and never let the
opposing team get their stick on the ball, then it'll be awesome,"
Rob said. "Any other scenario and it'll be a bloodbath. As far as
goalies go, Grant needs a lot of work."

"Yeah, me being goalie is not looking like a great idea."

"You'll be fine. Any goalie is better than no goalie. Besides,
this will be fun," Grady said. "Tomorrow we'll get you your
uniform and goalie equipment."

The team scattered in different directions. Most of the team
headed up the hill toward the student parking lot. TJ wandered
over to the bleachers mumbling something about finding some

girl, and Dax stayed on the field with the watch doing the first workout.

"Dax is probably heading to college on a football scholarship, so his workout numbers will be stellar." Grady nodded in Dax's direction. "Are you worried about your trainer figuring out you aren't doing your own workouts?"

"I'll tell her I had an espresso if she questions it." I wasn't worried. Even though I hadn't played team sports, I was a good athlete. "She's pretty smart. She'll figure it out before half the team has taken turns. But at least she can stop worrying before she gets pissed at me. Heck, maybe Will Smith will pull a muscle and distract her."

"Your trainer trains Will Smith?" Grady's eyes went wide. "That's pretty cool."

"Speaking of pretty cool..." Really dumb segue, but I needed information. "Do you know Bernie Jewell? What's her deal?"

"Bernie? Yeah, I know Bernie. What do you mean?" Grady asked, giving me the side-eye.

"Well, like does she have a boyfriend?"

"Not that I know of. I've been hanging around her more now because of Lacey." He shrugged. "I know she's nice and smart. I also learned she's ferocious if you hurt one of her friends."

"Yeah, I saw that Friday night." I'd gone to the talent showcase since Bernie had said she was going. Some fight between Lacey and Grady blew up. As near as I could tell, Bernie stepped in when it looked like Grady was going to bail on her best friend. "That was totally awesome the way she lit into you to protect Lacey."

"Ferocious Bernie makes me nervous, but I deserved it for sure." Grady ran a hand around his neck and grinned. "Are you looking to ask her out?"

I shrugged.

"Because you like her? Or is this for research?"

I opened my mouth to respond, but Grady cut me off.

"I'm going to have to tell you not to mess with Bernie if it's just research." Grady tipped his head toward a group of cheerleaders. "I've got some research for you. Go over there and ask Ashley out. She's the captain of the varsity cheerleaders."

"But I don't want to go out with her." The girl in question was pretty. She had a bright cheerleader smile and short shorts to show off her long legs.

"Not a problem. You're a nobody nerd. Just ask and you'll see." Grady gave me a push in the cheerleader's direction. "Go. Go and learn, king of the nerds. Haha, see what I did there?"

"Yeah, you're hilarious." I stumbled over with my gangly nerd stride, until I stood a few feet away from Ashley and her friends. She glanced at me and away again as she continued telling her friends about some new nail polish she wanted to try.

"Excuse me, Ashley?" I cleared my throat and pushed my glasses up with a finger at the bridge of my nose while I waited long seconds for Ashley to turn her head.

"Do I know you?" She raked her gaze down to my shoes and back again, looking very unimpressed. "Oh, are you the new guy from California?"

"Th-that's me." I looked down at my shoes before looking back into her face. "I was wondering if you'd like to go out. You know, with me."

"Oh honey, bless your heart." Ashley's attention snagged on one of the lacrosse players over my shoulder. "That's never going to happen. But you get points for trying."

Her friends snickered beside her and the snickers turned to outright laughter after I turned and walked away.

Grady grinned at me. "Bet you've never experienced that before."

"Nope. Can't say that I have."

7

GETTING "JUMPED" BY THE
AWKWARD NERD

Bernie

Tuesday after school

When the last bell rang at the end of seventh period, I followed the stream of kids out the front door into the late-winter afternoon. These were the days to appreciate before the black asphalt in the parking lot was hot enough to cook a pizza on.

I reached into the zippered pocket of my backpack for my car keys.

"Isn't it an amazing day?" Lacey said as we walked out to my car together. "The sun is shining, the birds are singing, and my cute pink flats made it through the day without scuff marks."

"I didn't think you could get any perkier, but you did." I fought the urge to both roll my eyes and grin. I was happy Lacey and Grady were a couple now. It was just that now that my best friend finally had time to listen to me complain about the things happening in my life—I couldn't stand to bring her down. What she and Grady had was too new. "I guess I can handle your brain on love."

"Looking good, Lacey!" some guy called out from the group of guys leaning up against a bright red Camaro.

Lacey was one of those perky, outgoing girls with friends in almost every clique in school. She was a joiner. She was president of the pep club and on the newspaper and yearbook staff. She dressed up for school in cute outfits, cute shoes, and cute hair styles. Pretty much my opposite.

"Who's the dude with you?" the guy called again.

Ugh. I notched up my chin and kept walking.

"Just ignore it," Lacey said, hooking her arm through my elbow, moving us past the jocks and over to my car.

That sounded like good advice because I was pretty sure the comments had come from John Ryan. Every time the guy opened his mouth it was clear he'd forgotten to pay his brain bill. "Like I care what a bunch of immature, shallow jocks think about me."

"Not all the jocks are jerks. TJ and Dax for instance." Lacey grinned. "Or Grady."

"I know." And I normally ignored guys like John Ryan but it seemed like I was having to ignore a lot of kids lately. I didn't understand why so many kids cared one whit what I looked like or that I didn't fit in. I mean, how did that affect them?

I opened my door and automatically lowered the side window to let fresh air in. Lacey did the same on her side while I removed the sun visor from the front windshield, tucking it behind the driver's seat.

My phone sounded with an incoming text, so I checked it since the only people who texted me these days were my grandmas, Lacey, Grant or work.

Yep, it was my manager texting the new schedule. I clicked the link to check and...*what the heck?*

"Unbelievable. They cut back my hours at work. And gave them to Todd." I threw myself behind the wheel and counted to three. Yes, Todd and I both worked at Al's Garage. Luckily we rarely worked the same days. "My manager knows I need the hours."

"Is this the same dude who hinted you weren't strong enough to handle the work?" Lacey snapped from the passenger seat, already affronted for me.

"Same dude. Of course, he didn't have the nerve to pull this when my dad was around." My dad had been the head mechanic of the garage for over ten years. Even though my dad tried to keep it from me, I knew there were a few employees who were unhappy about me working there.

"You don't want to hear this—and it's totally not fair—but I think you're going to have to prove you're just as good a technician as Todd." Lacey's gaze bored into mine. "You're going to have to enter the state competition again."

"No way. I'm not doing that."

"Bernie, tell me you aren't doubting yourself."

"I know I'm a good mechanic." I did. But that didn't mean my confidence hadn't taken a beating last year. I wasn't a glutton for punishment. If self-esteem were poker chips, my stack seemed to deplete daily. Last year's competition was me pushing all my chips into the pot, and that hadn't worked out at all.

"Do you?" Lacey frowned at me.

"Yes."

"Then why don't you fight for your job? Go talk to your manager. Or tell your dad what's going on."

"I'm not worrying my dad over this. His deployment is stressful enough."

"Okay, I get that. But the competition isn't *only* about proving you're just as good a mechanic as any guy." Lacey placed her hand on my forearm. "Are you forgetting the top finishers get scholarship money?"

Nope. That was the whole reason I'd entered last year. Tech school wasn't cheap and my blue-collar family had been living paycheck to paycheck for years. It had taken all of my mom's life insurance and Dad's savings to pay off mom's medical bills.

"Hang on, I just had a thought... Maybe my manager cut my hours because he's giving me the state inspection job I applied for." I knew Todd had applied for the job also, but I'd submitted my application first and had been working at the garage longer. "That would totally explain the change in my hours."

"Oh, okay. Then I'll allow your manager to live another day without getting his house TP'ed."

The image of Lacey with her good girl reputation tossing rolls of toilet paper into my boss's trees made me laugh as I inserted the key to start the car and...nothing.

"Oh, flippin' Froot Loops. Dead battery," I groaned. Dang it, I should have just asked Lolli for the money until I got my paycheck. "I'm sorry, Lacey. This is all my fault."

"It's okay. We'll just get a jump," she said before popping her head out the window and calling across the parking lot to the nearest group of guys. Just my luck, Todd Black was there. "Hey, guys! Would one of you give us a jump start?"

"Sure, Lacey. But only if you put it in the yearbook that Bernie asked me to jump her."

Ugh, John Ryan again. Idiot.

"No thanks, John." I leaned down to glare out Lacey's window at him. "I'd rather walk across the width of Texas with a handful of rattlesnakes and two scorpions in my pocket."

"I'll do it."

I turned to the voice out my window. *Grant.*

"Just give me a second to pull my car around." Grant straightened up from where he leaned against his Ford Focus.

"That would be great," I said.

Grant gave me a wink as he grabbed his keys from his pocket and slid into his car.

A wink? From Grant? *Aaaand* now my palms were suddenly sweaty. Sweaty palms simply because Grant was going to jump my dead battery? How dumb was that? Don't answer. I knew I was being ridiculous.

"You really should be better at vehicle maintenance, Bernard." Todd stood leaning against his Jeep Cherokee, enjoying the situation. "It's almost like you aren't a very good mechanic. Do you want me to let work know you're going to be late today?"

I narrowed my gaze at Todd who laughed in my face before jumping into his Jeep and peeling out of the parking lot.

Reaching down under my dash, I pulled the handle to unlatch the hood. I exited my car, walked around to the front, and slid my hand under the hood to depress the safety latch. Lifting the hood, I swung up the slender rod to hold it open, managing to poke myself in the eye in the process. *Ow. Nice move, Bernie.*

I tried to ignore Grant's car as it wound its way through the parking lot, but the closer he got, the more my nerves jangled. It was an awful lot like when I'd watched the movie *Jaws* with my brothers Brodie and Bryce a few summers ago. I'd had the same jangly-nerve feeling while watching the shark fin circle the swimmer, getting closer and closer and closer until—

"Bernie?"

"Yeah?" I blinked over at Lacey.

"Close your door so he can pull his car beside yours."

"Right." I blinked again to see Grant waiting about ten feet away from me, a small crooked grin on his face. Oh, boy. I darted around to shut my door and scooted out of the way as he pulled forward until his car sat two feet from mine. His engine cut, his hood unlatched with a pop, and then he was out and around the front end to lift the hood.

When he turned to look at me, prickly heat rushed over my face. What the heck? I saw the guy in class three days a week. So why was his brown gaze making me jumbled?

"Jumper cables? I know you have a set."

55

"Jumper cables?" I repeated, standing staring at him until Lacey elbowed me in the ribs. "Oh! Yes, jumper cables. In my trunk. Let me grab them." I spun around, moving down to the trunk of my car where I managed to hide my face for thirty seconds so I could pull myself together.

"Can't find them?" Grant asked from right next to me, which startled me into standing up so fast I hit the back of my head on the trunk.

"Ouch." Cheese and crackers that hurt. Rubbing one hand on the blossoming knot, I sucked in a breath through my teeth and refocused on the contents of my trunk. I ran my gaze over everything, hoping the cables were easily at hand so I could hurry this whole thing up. Except, there was a lot to look through: my grandma Gigi's accordion, a stack of books, a crate of old car parts for my lamps, my tool box, spare coveralls along with a change of clothes, a case of water, first aid kit, fire extinguisher, spare towels, and two rolls of duct tape because you just never knew.

"Wow. What are you, one of those end-of-the-world preppers or something?" Grant asked.

"There's nothing wrong with being prepared for a roadside emergency." I shot him a narrow-eyed glance. Sure the contents of my trunk said "Caution: Nerdy girl mechanic on board" but I wasn't embarrassed. Much.

"What's with the accordion?" His hand waved toward my trunk.

"It's a musical instrument." I wasn't going to get into the fact that I was such a dork that I was spending hours a week for a two-minute laugh for my grandma. I grabbed the stack of books out of the way, shoving them into Grant's hands so I could keep digging.

"*Fifty Shades of Grey?*" He read off the first title in the stack. "Interesting."

"It's not what you think it is," I said, mostly managing not to blush. It wasn't the famous erotica book. No, this *Fifty Shades of Gray* (notice the different spelling of "gray") was a cozy mystery book about a group of elderly women solving murder cases. I was reading it to the Book Babe Book Club at Shady Acres nursing home. I grabbed the book from his hands, shoved it back in my trunk and kept looking. "Ah ha! Here they are."

I held them aloft and that was when I realized one of the metal teeth clamps was caught on my "Girl Mechanics have Dirty...Hands" T-shirt which I was now waving around right in front of Grant's grinning face.

"Nice Tee," Grant said, adjusting his glasses as his smile widened.

"Uh...thanks." I unsnagged it, grabbed the rest of the books from Grant, and tossed everything back into the trunk before slamming it closed like I was hiding a dead body. Could I make this more awkward? Yes. Yes I could. Which was why I needed to stop acting weird around Grant. He was just being nice. It didn't *mean* anything.

I clenched my jaw before gritting out, "I'm ready."

Grant cleared his throat and held his hand out. "I'll just... I mean, should I..."

I stared at his hand, noticing how nice it was, you know, big and kind of athletic looking. I guess he was waiting for me to hand off the cables?

"I've got it," I said, moving around to the open hoods. In no time, I had the cables attached. (Both red clips to the positive terminals on each battery; one black clip to the negative terminal on Grant's battery and the second black clip to an unpainted bolt in my engine for grounding.)

Stepping back, I nodded over at Grant.

He'd been watching me with arms crossed over his chest and one cocked eyebrow.

"Do *not* tell me you're impressed." Yeah, we weren't talking rocket science here.

"Heck no. I know girls are just as capable as guys." Grant shrugged. "But part of me still likes getting to play the hero for the few seconds a strong independent girl like you needs one. And I don't mean that in some sexist way."

"Getting to play the hero?" He had swooped in and saved me from more of Todd's derision. Was it fate? Or just proof of how bad my days were going lately? "How is that not sexist?"

"Because... I'm more than happy to let you be my hero too." He leaned down until his head was right next to mine and whispered, "I'd trust you to save me any day of the week."

I blinked up at him, my breath stuck somewhere between exhaling and inhaling. I was in some crazy confused place I'd never been. I might have stood there forever if Grant hadn't turned me around and given me a gentle push toward my car.

We both got behind the steering wheels of our vehicles. His gaze caught mine through our open side windows and with a nod he cranked his engine on, gunning it a little to speed up the process. After a few minutes, I started my car. It took two tries to get the engine running, but it started. It looked like the universe was going to let me escape without embarrassing myself in front of Grant again.

"Who is that guy?" Lacey asked from the passenger seat, trying to look at Grant without staring.

"Um, that's the new guy in my auto shop class. I told you about him."

"You didn't tell me he was adorable."

Grant exited his car and carefully disconnected the cables.

She was right. I hadn't told her. I guess I sort of tried not to think of Grant as a guy because every time I did I got flustered. It was a little weird having a guy do me a favor. Especially with my car. My dad had made sure I was self-reliant. I was used to being independent and handling this kind of thing on my own.

Grant leaned around the hood and I gave him a quick wave of thanks when he called to me. His gaze was firmly on mine and he had that sweet smile again, the one that sort of distracted me whenever he sent it to me. Which seemed to be a lot.

I couldn't hear what he was saying over my running engine, so I quickly shut off my car.

I stuck my head out my driver's window. "I'm sorry, what did you say?"

Grant ran a hand over his mouth and dropped his head down to look at his shoes. When he lifted his head, his laughing eyes latched onto mine as he walked to bend down next to my window. "I said you need to keep it running for twenty minutes to recharge your battery. But I forgot you know that."

Fish sticks. He was right. I knew that. I freaking knew that but like the biggest idiot ever… I turned my key and…nothing.

I dropped my forehead to my steering wheel with a whimper.

"It's no big deal," Grant said. "It's just another chance to be a hero, right?"

"Right." I lifted my head from the steering wheel, pushed a few strands of hair off my face, and gave Grant a grateful nod while ignoring Lacey's giggle. "Thanks. I appreciate it."

"It'll take one second." Grant tapped his fist on my open window frame and moved back around, quickly reconnecting the cables to the appropriate terminals before sliding back behind his wheel and starting up his car. He revved it a few times, then glanced over at me. I nodded and started my car up for the second time.

I jumped out and removed the cables from both vehicles, slamming the hoods closed. After sending Grant another wave of thanks, I hustled back into my car, put it into drive, and exited the parking lot with a huge sigh.

"So that's your new auto shop partner," Lacey said.

"Yep. That's him. That's my shop partner." My voice was cool and matter of fact, but heat rushed over my cheeks. "The new guy. In my class."

"Oh my gosh!"

"Oh my gosh what?" I threw her a quick glance.

"You're blushing!" Lacey said.

"No. No I'm not." I totally was.

"Why Bernadette Jewell, since when have you had a thing for cute nerds?"

"I don't." I remembered his brown eyes looking at me, warm and serious. And that crooked smile like we shared a joke together—in a good way. Sure, he was cute in that awkward nerdy way. And he seemed nice. He was taller than me. Dark brown eyes—so intense—surrounded by the most ridiculously long eyelashes.

But it wasn't even that. It was that he didn't treat me like one of the guys. Or overlook me because I wasn't…well, girly.

"You don't?" Lacey sounded doubtful.

"I don't. I think I have a thing for boys who actually see me."

8

AN ALIEN ABDUCTION?

According to the tabloids... I was missing. This was expected. Although I'd hoped the paparazzi could have gone more than a week before whipping up a frenzy over the lack of a King sighting. The good news was there was nothing about Texas in the tabloids, so I still might get my full four weeks. I made a mental note to focus on staying below the radar while attempting to suck all the marrow out of my normal high school teenager experience. At the top of my list: find a way to spend more time with Bernie. My clock was ticking down and every moment I spent with Bernie felt real and necessary.

9

THAT'S NOT FAIR!

Bernie

I arrived at school early, so I had time to drop off my letter in the front office.

"Here you go, Mrs. G." I handed her the envelope. "Could you please see that—"

"Principal Barstow gets it. You know I will, hon." She grinned at me. "We're all rooting for you, you know."

"Bernie!" Mrs. Loftus poked her head from her office, disappeared, and then waltzed out with a bright smile on her face. She handed me a crisp sheet of paper. "I printed this out for you. It's a list of the available tech scholarships."

Guess what was at the top of the list? Yep, the Texas High School Automotive Technology Competition. *Aaargh.* Like I didn't know about that one. Luckily, there were a few more I could check out.

"Thank you for the list. I'll look into it tonight." I folded the paper in half and slid it into my backpack.

"Just a heads up, the deadline for the state competition closes out tomorrow," she said.

"Yes ma'am." It wasn't a deadline I needed to worry about. Been there, done that as they say.

After the office, I stopped at my locker to stash my lunch and then walked to shop class. Grant smiled at me from our table. I enjoyed Grant's company. He was nice, smart, funny and didn't treat me like one of the guys. Weird, right? When he looked at me—he just saw me—as I was. And he didn't seem to care that I wasn't like other girls. I loved that, but I also didn't know what to do with it.

Sometimes when he looked at me, a kaleidoscope of butter-flies took off in my chest—fluttering so wildly it was hard to breathe.

"Hey, Bernie." He held out a package of Red Vines. "Want some licorice?"

"Um, no thanks. Is that your breakfast?" Not that I was one to talk, since I usually ate Captain Crunch for breakfast when Lolli wasn't around.

"No. I had pancakes for breakfast and a muffin for second breakfast. The licorice is an early elevenses to tide me over until luncheon."

"Ah, you're a hobbit. That explains so much. Except you are way too tall to be a hobbit."

His eyes went wide behind his glasses. "You know *Lord of the Rings?*"

"I do. I'm a big LOTR fan. They're my favorite books."

Grant put a hand over his heart. "Has anyone told you that you may be the perfect girl?"

"*What?*" How in the world did he say that with a straight face? I darted a glance around, hoping no one else had heard that. I'd never hear the end of it if they had. Bernie Jewell, awkward tomboy, the perfect girl... Ha!

Luckily, Mr. Miles walked in and started class, so I didn't have to respond to Grant's comment.

"Pass your homework forward. Today everyone should be

THE TOMBOY & THE MOVIE STAR

moving on to the brake system's lab. If not, get moving." He held up a stack of forms. "Don't forget tomorrow is the last day to enter the state competition. Anyone need a form?"

I kept my eyes focused on the grease stain on my desk that looked like a space alien eating a taco.

"Moving on, let's all congratulate Todd. He got a state inspection job at his garage."

"*What?*" My gaze jerked over to Todd who sat waiting for my reaction. "You've got to be kidding. When?"

"Mike told me yesterday." Todd's face oozed into a smirk. "Aren't you going to congratulate me?"

"That's *not* fair." I hadn't meant to say that out loud but I was angry and frustrated and feeling like once again—no matter what I did—I'd always be excluded from their boy's club.

"Fair? Ha! What's not fair is forcing customers to let some diversity hire work on their car."

"Zip it, Mr. Black," Mr. Miles warned.

"Diversity hire? Who do you think you are?" I stood and stared Todd down. "You honestly think your Y chromosome makes you a better mechanic?"

"Absolutely. I'd say feel free to prove me wrong—but you're too chicken to enter this year's competition. You're afraid you'll lose again."

I wanted to wipe the smug look off Todd's face. I had to fight my urge to punch Todd in the face. Closing my eyes and counting to three, I heard Lacey's voice in my head. *You're going to have to prove you're just as good a technician as Todd. You're going to have to enter the state competition again.*

She was right.

"Mr. Miles, I'll take a form."

"That's the spirit. You'll need a partner and a signed permission slip by tomorrow."

Right. A partner. Last year I'd competed with Lisa, only she'd graduated. I ran my gaze around the room. The number of guys trying to avoid my eyes didn't bode well.

"Steve? Do you want to partner with me for the competition?" He was a good wrench. Near the top of the class.

"Can't. I already signed up to partner with Todd."

Figured.

"Sean?"

"Sorry, no."

"Joey?" I asked, but I already knew his answer. No guy in class was willing to cross Todd.

Joey shook his head, but at least he looked guilty about it. Some people just couldn't stand up to peer pressure.

"I'll do it," Grant said, quieting the laughter and chatter in the class.

I turned to Grant, staring into his sincere gaze remembering the times he'd almost killed our engine. Oh, man. Grant's car knowledge was weak, but I didn't have any other choice.

"Thank you." I nodded at him and then turned my gaze on Todd. "I'm in. And I will happily beat you and make you eat your words."

* * *

I was still fired up over Todd getting the inspection job at dinner that evening. Honestly, there was only one reason he got the job instead of me. And Lacey was right; I would have to prove I was as good a technician as Todd. After I beat him, I'd wave the first place certificate under their noses or hang it on the wall at the garage—so they couldn't deny I was a good mechanic.

"How was school?" Lolli asked as we finished her famous chicken pot pie.

"Fine. I need you to sign a permission slip for me." I grabbed the paper from my notebook on the counter and handed it to her. "It's for the state competition in two weeks."

"Good for you, Bernie." Lolli looked it over. "I'm happy to sign it...on one condition."

"What's that?" An unsettled feeling descended down my spine.

"If you enter the Miss Armadillo Pageant also." She notched her chin up and pursed her lips. "*And* you must give the pageant a real effort. The pageant is a week after the tech competition, so it won't interfere at all."

"That's blackmail, Lolli."

"Well, I'm sorry about that, but that's my condition," Lolli said. "Take it or leave it."

Todd's smirking face and bragging voice slithered through my head. Tension gathered in the pit of my stomach over getting passed over for a job I had earned. Yet, the pageant was a sure failure too. It was just that Lolli refused to accept that.

I was entering one contest to prove being a girl *wasn't* a handicap.

I was entering another contest where proving I *was girly enough* could win a girl a crown.

The irony was not lost on me. I was too girly and not girly enough. It was the story of my life. I didn't fit in anywhere.

I sucked in a deep breath and looked at Lolli. "I'll take it."

10

DID I DO THE RIGHT THING?

Grant

Thursday morning

"Do you think I did the right thing?"

"It sounds like this guy Bernie needed help, so yes." Mom slid the box of doughnuts I'd been eying across the counter to me.

"Bernie is a girl." I picked out a chocolate sprinkle doughnut before glancing back at my mom. "Actually...she's Bernadette Jewell."

Mom quirked her eyebrow at me. "Why am I not surprised? Tell me about her."

"She's serious and smart and passionate about cars and her friends. She's a fighter—like it's her against the world." I knew she had a best friend, but sometimes Bernie seemed very alone. Isolated. I wasn't sure if that was by choice or because kids could be so harsh. "She's strong. Sometimes she's the only one standing up to the bully in class."

"You like her." Mom raised her eyebrows at me. "You need to tell her who you are. It's not a secret you can keep forever, and it's better if she hears it from you."

I shrugged and stuffed about one-hundred grams of carbs of

doughnut into my mouth to avoid having to respond. My mom and I were close. But this was uncharted territory for me.

"I know. Just—not yet." I needed more time for her to get to know me. "About the tech competition…?"

"I think you did the right thing." Mom nodded, leaned over the counter and signed the permission form. "Without you, she can't compete, right?"

"Yeah, but my technical knowledge is weak. I could very well be a liability. I could be helping set her up for a big fall."

"I have never seen you fail at anything you've set your mind to." Her gaze held total confidence in me. "Now you can use that photographic memory of yours for something other than memorizing lines of dialogue."

"You're right. I can learn a lot in two weeks. Thanks, Mom." I grabbed my lunch from the counter and grinned at her. "I've got a quiz in English on King Lear. Wish me luck."

"Ha! We covered King Lear when you were in fifth grade." My mom had given up her teaching job when we moved to L.A. for my career. She'd been my tutor on the set up until freshman year when I needed more specialized tutors for advanced classes.

I was halfway out the door when I turned back. "Almost forgot—not to brag or anything—but I'm the new goalie on the varsity lacrosse team. Our first game is today."

"You really are fitting in everything you can in your four weeks, aren't you? You know I'll be there. Oh…" Mom's smile faded and her forehead creased. "Are you sure it doesn't violate your contract?"

I'd already signed the contract for the movie we'd film here in Texas. Every contract had a long line of prohibitions: no sky diving, no skiing, no race car driving, etc etc.

"Yep. Nowhere in the fine print does it say I cannot play on a high school varsity team. Besides, the goalie wears pads and a helmet."

"I can't wait to tell your father. He'll want to get here early to catch a few games." She sighed. "When you were little, he dreamed of watching his boy play sports. He'll love this."

Right. Another reminder that my parents had sacrificed many of their dreams to accommodate mine. And never once complained.

If you're thinking, yeah, tough sacrifice there, hot shot, giving up cheering for your mediocre high school athlete vs. the glamor of a movie star... Let me shut that down right now. My parents were salt of the earth folks. I mean, they were real. They were kind and hardworking. They weren't about money or fame or attending red carpet events or parties of famous directors. Dad played sports in high school and college. He loved sports. I know he'd have loved having a kid who played sports. Heck, he'd have been one of those dads who show up at every game wearing his son's jersey and ringing a cow bell.

So yeah, no matter how bad I was at goalie, my parents were going to love watching me play.

* * *

Since we didn't have shop class today, Bernie and I met in the cafeteria to eat lunch while we discussed how we'd approach studying for the competition. As soon as we stepped inside, Ro and Shani called across the large noisy room to me while Lacey waved Bernie over, but we shrugged them off and sat across from each other at an empty table in the back corner.

"Before we get started"—Bernie dumped her lunch bag out on the table in front of her—"I want to thank you for agreeing to be on my team."

"I've only been here at Jackson for two weeks, and I want to beat Todd. Even more, I want *you* to beat Todd." I dumped my lunch onto the table, and then reached across, raking her pile into mine before mixing them together. "I just hope I don't lose it for you. I will work my butt off over the next two weeks to make sure that doesn't happen."

"I'm going to owe you big." Her gaze caught on our food pile. "Wh-what are you doing?"

"It's like a picnic," I said. "We can count this as a first date."

"No, we can't." She shook her head, flicked her eyes toward me before picking her sandwich out from the pile. "Teenagers don't even go on 'dates' anymore."

"Or not." I reached out, snagging my double chocolate Pop-tarts. "Why don't you fill me in on how the competition works?"

"Sure. It's an all-day event divided into two sections. The morning session is the Workstation Challenge which accounts for sixty percent of our team's score. It's three hours of testing our knowledge of tools, measuring instruments, vehicle components, and job interview skills."

I placed the second Pop-tart down and moved on to my bag of kettle chips. "Pretty sure I can ace the job interview."

"Agreed. You're very outgoing and likable. And weirdly persuasive." Her gaze avoided mine.

"Are you saying you like me? As in like me-like me?" Part of me wanted to know and part of me was just teasing. But mostly I wanted to know.

"Moving on… The afternoon session is three hours of "hands on" challenge. Each team must diagnose and repair pre-staged problems under the car's hood." She took a chip when I offered her the bag, but instead of eating it, she slid it inside her ham sandwich and then took a bite. "The on-car session is timed and worth forty percent of our score."

"Timed. Worth forty percent. Got it." Darn, that ham and potato chip sandwich looked good. "Are you going to eat your whole sandwich?"

She shrugged, sliding over the plastic sandwich bag with the other half. "The good news is there are things we can focus on to gain points so we don't have to be perfect."

"Like?" I took a bite of the ham with potato chips and let me say it was as good as it looked. I hadn't had bread in four years and I couldn't get enough of this sweet, sweet miracle.

"Lots of teams lose points for not documenting everything onto the RO as they go. Time goes fast and there's never time to fill it out at the end."

"What's an 'RO'?"

"Repair order. If we forget to list a repair part on the RO—no points."

"That won't be us," I said. "I'm good with details and remembering things, so I can definitely help there."

"We can also score points by properly referencing the manuals during diagnostics. Some teams get flustered or cocky and skip steps."

"I'm all for proper referencing." I leaned forward, catching her eyes. "So, why can't we count this as a first date?"

"Because"—she blinked her green streaked eyes and her cheeks went pink—"um, because, you never asked me out."

"You're right. That's part of the process, isn't it? So it's a practice date while I gather my courage to ask you out." I opened the bag with my sandwich, handing half to Bernie. "You've got to try this. It's amazing."

She took a tentative bite and chewed, looked at the sandwich and then back at me as she swallowed.

"Well?"

"It's a peanut butter and jelly sandwich."

"Right? Darn good."

"I hope you won't take this the wrong way...but sometimes you seem a lot like an alien newly landed on earth."

"No offense taken." I grinned at her because, honestly, that was exactly how I felt navigating high school. And carbs. "Are you going to eat that fruit roll up?"

She handed it across carefully like you'd feed a hungry snake.

"So that's about it. We've got two weeks. There are seven

workstations, so we can cover one per day. That gives us a week to go over wiring diagrams and using measuring tools and diagnostics." She bit her lower lip before releasing a breath. "If you bailed now, I wouldn't blame you."

"Nope, I'm still in. We've got a good plan of attack. I'm busy tonight, but wide open from tomorrow night on." My mom and I had agreed to work on selecting this year's recipients for our ABG Foundation tonight. (I'd named my foundation for my parents, April and Brock, to honor them, but also so I could give back without attracting attention.) It was time-sensitive, so it couldn't be pushed back. "Does seven-thirty work for you?"

"Tomorrow at seven-thirty?" She nodded and sucked in a loud breath. "Yes. That works."

"Hey, what's the worst that can happen?" I smiled into her worried eyes.

"The worst? I lose to Todd, never get the job that should have been mine, don't get a scholarship for tech school which means I'll have to find a job until I save up enough money. Tech school isn't cheap and that's not even including purchasing a set of professional tools." She shoved a loose curl of sun-streaked brown hair from her face and gathered up the remnants of her lunch, dropping them back into her brown bag. "Other than that, nothing."

"Okay. That's a lot." I felt like an idiot that I hadn't understood that this wasn't just about some trophy. It wasn't really about Todd either. It was about fighting for what was right and for her future. "So we'll do everything in our power to win. That's all there is to it."

"You sound so confident and positive," she said.

"I've attempted things in my life people warned me were impossible. Lots of people." I reached across the table and took her hand in mine.

"What did you do?" she whispered, her gaze locked onto our joined hands.

"I did it anyway." I grinned. "I worked hard and ignored the people who said I couldn't."

If I had a dollar for every time someone warned me or my parents how many actors try to make it in Hollywood only to fail—well...I'd be a millionaire. Instead, I was a millionaire movie star because I *didn't* listen to all the naysayers.

"Yeah, but—"

I squeezed her hand gently to stop her. "Hey, have you forgotten the immortal words of Grandma Gigi? 'You've got to live through an experience in order to learn life's greatest lessons.'"

"Right," she said, pulling her hand away. "But I already lived through this once."

"Not with me as your partner, you haven't." I gave her a wink. "Hey, are you going to eat that Twinkie?"

She laughed and fished out the Twinkie for me. "Where are you putting it all?"

"I'll burn it all off in the lacrosse game today. Did I tell you I'm goalie?" I took a bite of the Twinkie, loving every cream-filled bite. "I've never played goalie before, so it might be ugly, but it'll be fun. You should come to the game."

"Lacey's going to 'ooh' and 'ah' over Grady, so I might tag along."

"Great. Feel free to 'ooh' and 'ah' over me all you want. Although the way I play it might be more of a 'boo' and '*ow*'."

Bernie

After school that afternoon, Lacey and I sat in the bleachers eating popcorn and watching our Jackson Jackalopes take on the Travis High Tornados. We sat up high and got caught up on each other's lives during the pre-game warm ups.

Lacey's update was easy since now that she and Grady were officially a couple, her life was even more sunshine, rainbows, and puppies than usual.

"Now fill me in on your life." Lacey turned all her attention to me. "You didn't call me, so I'm dying to know what happened with work. Did you get the inspection job?"

"Nope." I clenched my jaw, still feeling the anger and frustration over the situation. "The manager gave it to Todd."

"*What?* No." Lacey growled her frustration for me. "*Now* can we TP his house?"

"Ha! If I thought it would do any good… Looks like you were right about having to prove myself." I swallowed down the bitter unfairness of it. "So I entered the auto tech competition."

"Yes!" Lacey slapped her hands on her thighs. "Who did you get to partner with you? Steve? Joey?"

"Grant."

"Awesome. Is he better than Steve and Joey?"

"Not exactly. He's braver than Steve and Joey," I said.

"Ah, so he was the only guy in class willing to go against Todd? Good for Grant." Lacey's gaze moved over to Grant on the field and she gave him a thumb's up even though he wasn't looking. "I like this guy more every day. So, this is great."

"That's the good news..." I glanced at Lacey and away. "The bad news is the only way Lolli would agree to sign my permission slip was if I agreed to enter the Miss Armadillo Pageant. And actually try."

Lacey's head spun my way quicker than a rattlesnake strikes. "You're kidding!"

"I wish I was," I said. "Stop smiling, Lace. This is so not funny."

"It's sort of funny." She smothered a giggle but her lips were wobbling. "I can't help you with the tech competition, but I can totally help you with the pageant."

"I was hoping you'd say that. I mean, dresses, makeup, high heels and me do not compute. I love my grandma, but her obsession with this Miss Armadillo family tradition is unhealthy and bordering on unhinged."

"I'm sorry she's forcing it on you." Lacey pulled her planner from her purse and penciled my "pageant" training into her schedule. "I can come by your house in the evenings and we can spend time getting you prepared."

"Prepared? That sounds awful."

"Stop being a baby." Lacey poked my arm before grinning. "I'll be over after dinner tonight for our first session. It'll be fun."

I rolled my eyes before turning back to the field just as the game was ready to start.

It turned out, Grant was sadly right about his performance

as goalie. As the game progressed, the boos and groans over every goal that slid past Grant grew louder.

"Oh, man," Lacey said. "To be fair, I don't know much about lacrosse, but it looks like Grant is having a hard time."

"He needs to box out better. And he isn't swiveling his head fast enough." It was a fact that I'd played goalie more times than I could count when my brothers and their friends were short enough players. Everyone always wanted to shoot on the goal, so I was always stuck being goalie. As a matter of pride, I worked at it and became darn good. Not many guys could get a ball past me. "The Tornados found his weak side in the second quarter and they're attacking it. If it weren't for Grady, Dax, and TJ controlling the ball so well, this would be very, very ugly."

"Grady is good, isn't he?" Lacey sighed.

"He and Dax are good, but TJ's got the best stick," I said, keeping my gaze glued to the breakaway play on the field. "Look at him change hands to avoid the defenders. Oh wow, did you see that?"

"Did TJ just shoot that goal from behind his back?" Lacey asked with the appropriate amount of awe in her voice, even for someone who didn't totally understand the game.

"Yep." I watched Grady and TJ leave the field as Josh came on for the face-off. Grady was the better face-off man, but he needed a rest. Which meant, I hoped Grant was ready. He shifted from foot-to-foot in front of the goal, like he knew what was coming his way. Sure enough, the Tornados won the face-off and proceeded to run the ball down field, behind the goal, and shoot and score on Grant's weak side. "Oh, boy."

The Jackalopes lost 21-9.

Lacey pulled me down to the sidelines so she could talk to Grady. Weirdly, Grady wasn't upset about the loss at all. He had his arm around Grant's shoulders and was grinning ear-to-ear. Grant, on the other hand, wasn't grinning. He was apologizing to Grady and whatever other teammate was nearby.

"I'm sorry about that." He tugged his helmet off and ran a frustrated hand through his sweat-matted blond hair, making it stick up like a mad scientist. "That loss was all me. I'll get better. I promise."

"Hey, the opponent has to get past nine other guys to get to you," Grady said. "The blame isn't all yours."

"Mostly mine." Grant's lips compressed into a firm line and his jaw clenched. Obviously, he took losing to heart.

Lacey and Grady wandered off. Dax and TJ each slapped Grant on the back in solidarity before heading inside. There were a few guys on the team who sent Grant frustrated glances. Chad was outright rude with his glare and his passive-aggressive mumbling, *"Way to lose the game nerd-nozzle"* under his breath as he walked away, but Chad couldn't play either, so he had some nerve being all judgy McJudge-face.

Grant let out a heavy breath as he focused his gaze on me. "Well, that went about how I thought it would. Although, it came at me faster than I expected, you know?"

"I know." I'd faced down ninety-mile-an-hour shots many times before.

"It would have been fun to win, but mostly, I feel bad for letting the team down." He frowned. "I've been on a team of sorts before—not a sports team—but, you know, projects that take group effort. I've always pulled my weight. Always. This time, not so much, and I don't like it."

"Remember at lunch when I said I would owe you real big for helping me?" I glanced at him as he settled at my side as we walked off the side-lines toward the parking lot. "I can help you with playing the goalie position."

"I don't want to cut into our study time." Grant shook his head. "There's no way I want to hurt our chances of winning the auto competition."

"It won't. It's not that you're not athletic." I glanced away, ignoring the heat sneaking into my cheeks. Yeah, I'd watched him practically the whole game. I'd had a hard time pulling my gaze off him even for some of Grady's or TJ's stellar plays. "I think you only need a bit of coaching on how to play the position. And more time in front of the goal while someone's shooting on you. Come over to my house at seven instead of seven-thirty tomorrow and we'll fit in some practice first."

"I'd appreciate it, but if it ends up cutting into our competition prep, then we stop. Deal?"

"Deal." I was touched that he was putting my tech competition before his desire to win.

"And just throwing this out there…if you wanted to extend me a dinner invitation a few evenings—considering the fact that I'll be at your house for hours and hours for the next two weeks"—he gave me a side-eyed innocent look—"I wouldn't turn you down."

"You wouldn't, huh?" I turned my face forward, but couldn't stop my lips from sliding into a grin. "I'll check with my grandma Lolli, but I'm pretty sure that could be arranged."

"Dinner, sports, and car talk. Sounds like a date…"

"Still not a date." I knew he was joking. He had to be, didn't he? Either way, it was smart to keep it simple. We were two friends helping each other. It was smart to draw that line. What would be stupid would be thinking crazy things about Grant…and me.

"What about a dress rehearsal for a date?"

"Still no." But there went the stupid butterflies flitting through my chest and through my veins.

12

I'LL TELL YOU, BUT YOU CAN'T LAUGH

Grant

Friday, the next day at school

Walking into the cafeteria was one of my favorite things. It had been over ten years since I could walk into a crowded space and not be recognized. I loved my fans—but I was savoring every minute of being a normal teen.

I found Bernie sitting at "our" table in the far back corner. Lacey sat next to her and they both stared at Lacey's phone. Lacey looked enthusiastic (normal from the little I'd known her) but the look on Bernie's face could only be described as...horrified.

"Everything okay, Bernie?" I slid onto the bench opposite her.

"Everything is fine," Lacey responded. Swiping her finger across her phone's screen. "What about this one?"

"Nope."

Swipe. "This one?"

"Nope."

Swipe. Sigh. "This one?"

"No way."

"What's going on?" I asked, my gaze moving back and forth between the girls before settling on Bernie.

"Torture," Bernie said. "Maybe even grandchild abuse."

"Come again?" I arched an eyebrow but Lacey only snickered and bumped her shoulder against Bernie's.

"Oh, stop. You're such a baby." Lacey rolled her eyes.

"It's a dress." Bernie shot Lacey a narrow-eyed glance. "With ruffles."

"It's adorable is what it is," Lacey said, glancing back at the phone with a happy smile.

"Sure it is. On you. Or any other girl," Bernie grumbled. "Not on me."

"A dress? What's it for?" I leaned forward trying to get a look at the horrible, ruffled dress assaulting Bernie's dignity.

Bernie huffed out a breath. "I'll tell you, but you can't laugh."

"Why would I laugh?" I asked, darting my gaze to Lacey and back to Bernie's frowning face.

"And you can't tell anyone."

"I will take it to my grave." I lifted my hand, palm out, next to my head.

"I'm a contestant in the Miss Armadillo Pageant." Bernie's sharp gaze dared me to laugh or smile.

Obviously there was a story here but one glance over at Lacey's discrete headshake told me now was not a good time to ask about it. "Ah, okay. Well, I think ruffles are the wrong way to go. Definitely not you."

Lacey arched an eyebrow at me. "You know women's fashion?"

"No." Honestly, I sort of did. Fashion played a big part in Hollywood: wardrobe for movies, getting decked out for the red carpet or some big party, or even not looking bad when some paparazzi jumped out from behind a trash can to snap a photo. One of my closest friends in the business was actress Talia West. We'd attended the Oscars and the Teen Choice Awards the last three years together and had to coordinate what we wore for the red carpet. Yeah, I knew a little something about women's fashion. "Just trying to help by sharing a guy's opinion."

"I appreciate any opinion that agrees with me on no ruffles," Bernie said, lifting her hand so we could fist bump across the table. "Ixnay on the ruffles, Lace."

"But—"

"Also, I'm not petite like you. I wear a 10 or 12 depending on how form-fitting it is."

Bernie was tall for a girl and built like a strong athlete. Maybe that height and size made her feel awkward, but she reminded me of a few of the stunt women I knew in the business. A combination of muscle, bone, and sheer perseverance.

"Not a problem. I'll run by Chloe's Consignment Closet and grab some dresses for you to try on tonight." Lacey scrolled through her phone looking at more pictures. "Chloe posts her new arrivals on her website and there are some definite ruffle-free contenders. I guarantee I'll find a dress for you."

"Oh, heck. I'm being a brat." Bernie puffed out a breath and sent Lacey a lopsided grin. "I really appreciate your help. As long as it fits, it doesn't matter what the dress looks like."

"Only a little bratty, but I get it. You fought the good fight with Lolli for years, so it's frustrating to lose this late in the game." Lacey wrapped an arm around Bernie's shoulders and squeezed a quick hug. "I'm going to get us some cookies. Any requests? Chocolate chip? Oatmeal?"

"Chocolate chip," Bernie said.

"Cookies?" That perked me right up. "I'll take a peanut butter cookie if they have any."

"Got it." Lacey spun away toward the cafeteria line.

"I'm being dumb, I know." Bernie stabbed a straw into her milk carton. "It's just—"

"Hey, you don't need an excuse. You've got a lot on your plate. I get it. We've got this." I leaned forward, looking directly into her eyes. "First, we'll win the Texas High School Auto Tech Competition and then you'll be crowned Miss Armadillo."

"*Whoa, no.*" Bernie's face couldn't look more horrified if a cockroach had run across the table. "I only need to enter the pageant. I promised Lolli I'd take it seriously, but that doesn't mean I need to try to win it. That's like tilting at windmills anyway, so no."

"Okay." I nodded. She was totally selling herself short, but the look on her face said this might not be the best time to share my opinion. "So, lose Miss Armadillo. Win the auto competition. That should take some pressure off you."

"You obviously don't know my grandma."

"The infamous Grandma Gigi of the wise words?"

"No. Other grandma. Grandma Lolli, the true believer in all things that make a southern belle: big hair, pageants, and milk bath facials."

"Milk bath facials?" Hey, I'd heard weirder beauty treatments in Hollywood. A lot weirder.

"She swears by them. Don't get me wrong—my grandma Lolli is wonderful. She's sweet and adorable. It's just that she goes crazy over this pageant stuff."

"So we like Grandma Lolli…"

"We love Lolli. We just hate pageants."

"Okay. For the next two weeks, I'm team Bernie. I'm here to help you any way I can." I pointed at her. "You can count on me."

"I appreciate it." Bernie pulled out a stack of papers, sliding them into the middle of the table between us. "I printed out the diagrams of each major system. If it's okay with you, tomorrow we can start eating lunch in shop class while we work. We're still on for tonight at my house, right?"

"Yep."

"Oh, heck. I just realized it's Friday." Bernie shook her head. "I'm an idiot. I can't ask you to blow your Friday night studying."

"I'm a nerd, remember? I can't think of anything I'd rather do than spend Friday night studying with you." That wasn't a lie or an exaggeration. Which was sort of a revelation to me.

"Right." Bernie's shoulders relaxed and she sent me a crooked smile.

We spent the rest of lunch studying the diagram of the transmission system. Basically, Bernie gave me a "TED Talk" while I committed the diagram to memory.

"I'm back." Lacey plopped down at the table, sliding two peanut butter cookies over to me. "And I dragged Grady with me."

"I'd follow you anywhere, babe." Grady slid in next to Lacey with a wide grin. He reached across and snagged one of my cookies.

"Hey!" I shoved the other cookie in my mouth before he could grab that one too.

"Did you guys hear that Kingsly Grant is missing?" Lacey leaned into the table, wide-eyed.

Missing? I almost choked on the cookie, but managed to swallow it down. Sure I'd seen the tabloid headline the other day, but who believed those? I really hoped that the story hadn't been picked up by a major news outlet. That would be bad.

"Who?" Bernie sent Lacey a distracted glance.

"Kingsly Grant," Lacey said. "You know...King...the movie star? I just heard it from Gwen who said she heard it from Josh."

Grady's glance slid to mine before he laughed and said, "Maybe consider the source... Let's remember that Josh believes in Bigfoot and thinks burping out our school fight song attracts girls."

"I considered that," Lacey said. "But it's all over the internet too."

Bernie blinked. "Is that the guy the TV crew was asking about a couple weeks ago?"

"Yes." Lacey's gaze met mine and she tilted her head and

narrowed her eyes. "Has anyone ever told you that you look a little like King?"

"Do I? I'll take that as a compliment." I pushed my glasses up with a touch of my finger on the bridge and jutted out my jaw. "I saw him in *Seventeen Summers* and he was pretty jacked. Maybe I should see if he needs a body double."

That had Lacey's gaze roaming over my sweat shirt. Today I was wearing one with a picture of Einstein saying "You Matter. Unless You Energy."

"Dude, she said a *little* like him." Grady practically busted a gut over the idea, which I'd thank him for later. "Not to be mean, but body double might be stretching it. I mean, maybe in some parallel universe where King is a super-nerd who's out-of-shape and awkward, then sure."

13

OH, BUT YOU WILL, GRASSHOPPER

Grant

After parking on Bernie's driveway, I grabbed my goalie stick and a bag of balls from my car, setting them on the front walk before I climbed the well-worn wooden steps up to Bernie's porch. There were two comfortable-looking rocking chairs on the porch, one occupied by a woman with her silver-streaked hair piled high into a Texas-sized updo. She had a knitting project forgotten in her lap as she peered in through the open window next to her.

"You must be Bernie's Grandma Lolli," I said.

Her head whipped toward me and one hand flew to her throat while the other knocked the knitting off her lap.

"Sorry. I didn't mean to startle you." I thought she'd have heard my car pull down the gravel driveway. I retrieved the knitting, handing it over to her. "I'm Grant. I believe Bernie's expecting me."

"Yes, yes. Bernie said you were coming by." Lolli leaned back to the window and called, "Bernie, your special friend is here!"

From inside, there was a squeak as something fell with a splat and then a snicker.

"Everything okay?" I called inside. "Need help?"

"No! Everything's fine!" Bernie called back. "Except for the fact that I'm eighteen years old and have been walking wrong my whole life!"

I cocked at eyebrow at Lolli, hoping she'd clear up that mystery.

"Lacey's helping Bernie practice walking for the pageant." Lolli's gaze moved to the window and she sighed. "I offered my help, but as you might know, Bernie can be very...independent."

I did know that about Bernie. Grandma Lolli's face was full of love and pride but also something else I couldn't quite put my finger on. Yearning?

Bending down to peer into the window, I winked at Lolli before calling inside, "Bernie, let's see it. Come out and show us your walk. We promise not to judge."

"I don't mind judging," Bernie said, pushing her way through the screen door with Lacey right behind her. "It's the laughing I don't care for."

"I already said I was sorry," Lacey said. "And I wasn't laughing at the way you walked but at the expression on your face. You looked like I was forcing you to walk over pus-filled lizards in bare feet."

"Okay, that's gross." Bernie's face pinched up. "Fine. Maybe the shoes and the book on my head aren't so bad. Let me find my inner-girl—surely I've got one—and try again."

"That's our girl," Lacey said, sending a thumb's up over to Lolli.

"Shoulders back and lead with your hips," Lacey directed.

Bernie took a breath, placed the book on her head, shifted her hips forward and proceeded to walk the length of the porch as if she were walking on slippery ice. During an earthquake.

"Well, it's better," Lacey said, nodding her encouragement. "Wouldn't you agree, Grandma Lolli?"

"Oh my, yes," Lolli said enthusiastically, although her face didn't quite match.

"What if you kept your gaze higher and focused more on your feet instead of your hips?" I suggested. What can I say? Even male actors had to learn how to move. High definition cameras picked up everything.

"I don't mean to be a wise-ass, but how about you demonstrate that..." Bernie held the book out to me.

"Sure." I took the book, moved down to the opposite end of the porch, placed the book on my head, stared directly into Bernie's eyes and walked from one end of the porch until I stood three feet in front of her. "Of course, I'm not wearing heels, but you get the idea. And I don't believe for a second you didn't mean to be a wise-ass."

"You know me so well." Bernie shrugged.

"Um...that was—wow." Lacey gave me the once-over. "You just floated across the porch."

"That was perfect," Lolli said. "Graceful and elegant."

"Fine," Bernie said. "Never let it be said that I'm not up to a throw down. Let me try your way."

"That's the spirit." I handed her the book and backed up to the opposite side of the porch. "Alright, let's see it. Bring it, Jewell."

She placed the book on her head, pinned me with her gaze like I was her target and she was a dart, and walked toward me. It wasn't graceful and elegant. Bernie's long strides were confident, athletic, and full of barely contained energy. Not going to lie, it was pretty hot.

When she stood in front of me, she tilted her head forward and the book fell into my hands.

"How was that? Better?" she asked.

"Hmmm." Lolli blinked and tilted her head to the side.

"Not better?" Bernie's shoulders slumped and her gaze ran around to each face on the porch.

"You're a work in progress," I said. "Just like me and my goalie skills."

"Exactly." Lacey flashed Bernie an encouraging smile. "We'll keep working on it. Now go try on the dresses I brought."

"Do I have to? I don't want to keep Grant waiting. I promised we'd get in some lax practice before we study."

"It'll take less than ten minutes." Lacey rolled her eyes. "I only brought three to start."

"I've got all night." I took the rocking chair next to Lolli, stretching my legs out to relax. "Let's see the dresses."

Lacey almost had Bernie convinced to try on the dresses when Grady pulled his truck onto the driveway.

"Thank goodness. Grady for the save," Bernie said as he walked up the drive to stand with one foot perched on the bottom porch step.

"How awesome am I? You're welcome." Grady puffed out his chest taking a Superman pose. "What did I save this time?"

"Don't encourage him," Lacey said, but sent a pretty encouraging smile to her boyfriend.

"You saved all of us," Bernie said. "Honestly, I was about to be a major pain in the butt and this is a much-deserved time out. No one should have to suffer through me trying to be a girl."

"Hey, now..." Lacey gave Bernie a firm look. "You do need a break with a comment like that. Do you and Grant want to come to the drive-in with us? They're having a Kingsly Grant marathon in an attempt to get him to pick Jackson High as his next movie location."

"What drive-in?" Bernie frowned. "Coyote Tom's Drive-In has been closed for years."

"Coyote Tom passed away and willed it to his son." Lolli shook her head and pursed her lips. "But Tom, Jr. cheated on his wife and went through a messy divorce which dragged on for years. His ex-wife finally got it in the divorce settlement and fixed it up and this is the grand re-opening. Only now it's called Coyote Tom's Son's Ex-Wife's Drive-In."

"You're kidding about the name." Not that I thought someone's pain was funny, but the actor in me loved the name of the drive-in.

"No. Like I said, it was an ugly divorce."

"You in?" Grady asked, smirking at me. "I mean, I've heard King's acting is a little weak but the car chases are awesome."

"Grant and I are studying tonight," Bernie said.

"I don't think he's *that* bad of an actor," I said, which only made Grady's smirk grow wider. "Lacey seems to appreciate him."

"What's not to appreciate about King without his shirt on?" Lacey asked. "Duh."

I laughed as Grady's smirk morphed into a grimace and then he sent me a subtle nod before he reached for his girlfriend's hand.

"Fine, Lace. Shirtless King for you and car chases for me." Grady wrapped his arm around Lacey's shoulders and led her down the driveway, calling over his shoulder, "We're off to have fun. Enjoy studying, you crazy nerds."

"It was nice meeting you, Grant." Lolli gathered her knitting and stood. "I'm going to head in to watch *Murder She Wrote*. Sometimes I get lucky and find an episode I haven't seen."

She wandered inside, the screen door closing with a soft whoosh behind her leaving just me and Bernie on the porch.

"Time to work on your goalie skills." Bernie kicked off her high heels and shoved her feet into a pair of well-worn sneakers next to a big planter of geraniums. "Ready?"

"Absolutely. I hate being the reason my team loses the game."

We walked around her house and back toward the detached garage where a full-sized lacrosse goal sat up against the side of it.

"You won't need your stick to start," Bernie said, picking up three tennis balls from a pile of lacrosse supplies in the grass. "How's your juggling?"

"My juggling? How does that—" I stopped talking when Bernie began juggling the tennis balls like a pro—"Whoa. That's impressive."

"Your turn." Bernie tossed the tennis balls to me one at a time. "You can start juggling with two balls if you like or three if you can handle it."

"Challenge accepted." I had juggled before. Filming a movie and TV show required a lot of time on a set. A lot of boring downtime especially for a child actor. So in between all my tutoring we also did things to stay amused: puzzles, board games, crosswords, a lot of hands of go fish, close-up magic, and juggling—you name it I'd done it.

I tossed the balls in the air one after another and juggled. Sure I was a little rusty, but it didn't take me long to find and settle into a rhythm. Each time I dropped the ball Bernie would toss it back into the mix.

"Not bad," Bernie said.

"I think what you meant to say was awesome job."

Bernie laughed and shook her head.

"You know you want to." I let the tennis balls fall at my feet while I shot her a smile.

"If that's what you need to hear, awesome job, Grant. Time to catch some cards."

"I don't see what juggling and a deck of cards have to do with playing lacrosse."

"Oh, but you will, grasshopper." Bernie grinned at me. "You will."

She grabbed a deck of cards from her pile of supplies, flipped a large plastic industrial bucket upside down and stood on it. "I'll flip the cards at you one at a time and you try to catch each one. Focus on driving with your top hand and stepping forward with your lead foot toward the card."

"All I have to do is catch the cards?" It sounded almost too easy.

"That's it. Take your goalie stance in the crease. Ready?"

"Absolutely. Maybe soon we'll get on to something challenging."

I probably should've kept my mouth shut. Bernie started flicking the cards at me and let me just say it was harder than I thought it would be.

"Drive that top hand quicker. Faster lead foot. The *other* lead foot."

"I'm trying!" I laughed at my own incompetence but focused. *Drive the top hand. Forward lead foot. Top hand. Lead foot. Drive. Step. Drive. Step.* "Okay. I think I'm getting it."

"You are. Keep your eyes on the card."

When we got to the end of the deck, I stopped to catch a breather and looked around at all the cards I'd missed scattered on the ground. "Looks a lot like when we were little kids and played 52 pick-up."

"Actually, that's pretty good for your first time. Good job, Grant." Bernie's gaze met mine. "You're very athletic and you've got excellent eye-hand coordination."

"Ah…eye-hand coordination. I see the method to your madness."

Bernie jumped off the bucket and together we gathered the cards, set them to the side, and grabbed a lacrosse stick and a bucket of balls.

"Now grab your goalie stick and you'll see how it all comes together."

I stood in front of the goal and took my stance.

Bernie tilted her head before giving it a shake. "I'm thinking a helmet might be a good idea." She moved back over to her pile of supplies and pulled a helmet out of an old canvas bag and tossed it to me. "It's one of my brothers so it should fit."

Considering my mother and my agent and the movie studio

would be less than thrilled if I showed up with a black-eye or a concussion, I happily agreed with Bernie and took the helmet, strapped it on and retook my goalie stance.

"This is called quick stick. I'll shoot the ball at you and your goal is to stop as many as you can. Here's where the juggling and the cards come in... It's the same principles. Keep your eye on the ball, drive your stick with your top hand, and step toward the ball."

With that, Bernie stepped on the end of a nearby lacrosse stick, making it pop up in the air where she grabbed it and scooped up a ball.

"Ready?" She waited for my nod and then like a machine started shooting ball after ball at me.

We started off slowly so I could think about all the moving parts. The more shots Bernie took, the better I understood and the better I got.

"That's it. Good eye, Grant."

Praise from Bernie was high praise for sure. Because the more we practiced, the more I realized Bernie was easily as good a lacrosse player as some of the better players on the team.

In fact, at one point I got so distracted watching Bernie I totally missed seeing a ball take a bad bounce, sending it at me fast and low. *Ouch.* Right in the crotch hard enough to drop me to my knees.

"Yikes, sorry about that," Bernie said. "That one took a wicked hop. Are you okay?"

"I will be in a second." I bent over with my hands on my knees to catch my breath. "So a helmet was a great idea, but a cup would've been better."

"Oh, double yikes." Bernie began collecting all the balls by scooping them up in her stick and tossing them into the bucket. "Sorry about that."

"Not your fault at all. Totally my fault." I stood back up, turning my head to look at Bernie. "I didn't take into account what a good athlete you are. If I had, I would've had all my protective gear on. And that's on me."

"With four older brothers, I played a lot of sports with boys. Boys who gave no quarter because I'm a girl. I learned not to cry real fast."

Was that why Bernie came off so tough and independent?

"Do you want to practice some more?" Bernie asked.

"No. I'm good." I laughed, leaning down to help her gather the rest of the lacrosse equipment. "Seriously, I feel like I learned a lot. Let's move to the garage and focus on our competition. That's our main goal and I don't want to short change that."

14

WHERE THE MAGIC HAPPENS

Bernie

"Sweet garage." Grant stood next to me, taking everything in. "My dad's a mechanic. He used to run his shop out of this garage until he invested in a shop in town."

I ran my gaze around the three-car garage. The wall to my right held all our tools. There were two large deep red craftsman tool chests, a line of old kitchen cabinets that held oil, grease, gas cans and paint. On the back wall were three deep wooden shelves which held car parts; one shelf for each of our project cars. The wall to the left contained a well-used oil-stained workbench which right now was filled with my mess. Tucked in next to the workbench was a sink, an old ancient refrigerator and an old love seat of Lolli's covered in lilac cabbage roses.

"Is your dad at work? I'd like to meet him."

"My dad's in the Reserves and they just left on a deployment to Iraq. That's why my grandma Lolli is staying with me."

"That's cool." Grant shook his head at my raised eyebrows. "I don't mean cool he's gone. That must be tough on you. I mean cool he's in the military."

"My dad and I are close, so yeah, I miss him when he's gone."

"Nice Vette." Grant said. He walked over and ran his hand along the tail end. "She's a beauty."

"That's my dad's latest project car."

"Whoa. What's that?" Grant asked, his attention caught on something new as he moved toward the workbench. "Is it a lamp?"

"Yeah."

"It looks like... Is it made out of car parts?" He picked one table lamp up, turning it around to examine it before turning to look at me. "You made this. These are the parts you had in your trunk. This is...amazing."

"They're not amazing. They're just lamps. Made with car parts. I just—I mean, I was teaching myself to weld and a couple people liked them. So now I sell them to pay for car parts."

"They're not *just* lamps, Bernie. They're works of art. They're cool and retro yet modern and industrial. How much do you sell them for?"

"Twenty-five for the small lamp, and fifty for the large."

"You could charge a lot more. You *should* charge a lot more." He set the lamp down and picked up a smaller one. "I'll buy this one."

"I'm not letting you buy a lamp. Not after everything you're doing for me." I shook my head. "You can have it."

"Thank you. But I might need to buy more for gifts. I know a few people who would love these."

"Oh, okay." I wasn't going to turn that down. Car parts and car maintenance weren't cheap. And whatever I had leftover I put away to save toward tech school. I knew my dad would try to help me all he could. But after years of living under the weight of Mama's medical bills, the last thing I wanted to do was let my dad take on more debt because of me. I walked over and opened the hood on my old Ford truck. "Ready to get going?"

"I was born ready." He walked over until we stood side-by-side looking down into the engine. "This is nice. Is it a '55 F-100?"

"Good eye. This is my starter project. I've learned almost everything I know about engines by working on this truck." Dad and I had spent many hours in here with him teaching me about cars. It had been a way for us to keep moving forward. A way for us to ground each other without having to expose emotions neither one of us was ready to deal with. "As soon as I have enough money to get Earl the paint job he deserves, he'll become my daily driver."

"Earl, huh?" Grant grinned at me. "I can respect that. He looks like a solid workhorse."

I smiled up at him, enjoying that he got it. Poor Lacey never understood my relationship with Earl.

"I thought we could start by going over the transmission system we studied at lunch today," I said, dragging my gaze away from his.

"Sure, but I've got it."

"What do you mean you've got it? You only looked over the chart for ten minutes yesterday."

"I mean I've got it." He leaned his forearms on the truck and pointed into the engine. "The oil pan is at the bottom of the crankshaft and stores the engine's oil. The oil pan is connected to the oil pump which pushes the oil through the filter and squirts it on the crankshaft. The timing belt coordinates the movements of the camshaft and crankshaft. The valve train is made up of valves, rocker arms, pushrods, and lifters. How am I doing so far?"

"Um...great. Perfect so far."

"I told you I had it. Moving on to the combustion chamber..."—he turned and wiggled his eyebrows at me with a grin—"That's where the magic happens."

"M-magic?" I blinked at him, distracted by his brown eyes and his lopsided grin.

"Oh yeah. Fuel, air pressure and electricity come together creating a small explosion. Should I go on?"

Apparently when this adorable nerd talked about cars it created a small explosion in my chest, blowing my lungs apart until it was impossible to breathe.

"Nope. Nope, you've got it." *Breathe, Bernie, breathe.* "It sounds like you know more about cars than I thought. Which is great."

"Yeah, about that... I wish that were true, but the truth is I have a photographic memory. So, I don't have a lot of car knowledge yet, but I will in two weeks." He pushed his glasses up on his nose and gave me a firm look. "You can count on me."

The weird thing was I did count on him. I totally trusted that he would do everything he could to help me. And I didn't trust easily. A sad side-effect of people exiting my life when I wasn't ready, not that either my mom or my dad had a choice.

I lost track of time after that. Together, Grant and I started digging into the engine, talking through different systems, and bringing up scenarios of diagnosing and repairing different problems. We spent some time rolling around underneath Earl, stretched out on wheeled-creepers with a shop light hanging from the front axle. We explored from above, bent over with our hands elbow-deep in Earl's engine.

"I don't know about you, but I'm ready for a break," Grant said, grabbing a rag to wipe some of the grease from his hands.

I jerked my gaze from Grant to Dad's clock on the wall with wrenches as arms. "Wow, is it after eleven? Yikes! I'm sorry."

"Hey, no worries. I'm enjoying this. It's just my back muscles are screaming at me." He lifted his arms high, stretching out the muscles in his back. "Obviously, this nerd needs to work out more."

"It's not you." I moved to the sink and began scrubbing my hands with the lava soap. "It sort of goes with the job some days."

Grant joined me at the sink and I handed him the soap. He scrubbed his hands next to me, his arm bumping up against mine before he took his turn under the flow of water as soon as I finished.

Stepping away, I dragged a rag over my face and neck.

"You, uh, missed a streak," he said, his gaze on my face. "On your cheek."

I scrubbed the rag back over my cheek. "Better?"

"No." He grinned and stepped close, He took the cloth from my hand and gently ran it across my cheek. "There."

"Thanks." I quickly pulled away, sticking my face into the fridge to cool my heated cheeks for a few seconds before grabbing two waters from the fridge. I handed one to Grant and sagged onto the loveseat.

Grant relaxed down next to me, tilting his head back to polish off half his water in a few swallows.

"Can I ask you a question?" He turned to face me, stretching his arm along the back of the couch. "Why do you need this so much?"

"You've heard Todd." I blew out a frustrated breath, sending loose curls of hair off my face. "Because I need to prove that I'm as good a mechanic as a guy."

"Won't passing a certification test do that?"

"Yes. No. I just..." I clenched jaw, trying to find the words to explain.

"Just what?"

"I'm tired of being told I don't belong. I don't belong working on cars because I'm a girl. I don't belong in the girl's bathroom because I'm not girly enough."

"*What?* Are you telling me girls give you a hard time using the bathroom? That's so not cool. And it's not right. Who would do that?"

"*Gah.* I don't want to talk about it. I'm just—I'm tired of feeling like I never fit in anywhere." So tired that I'd stopped trying a long time ago. But that hadn't made the feeling of being an outsider go away. It was a lonely place to be. And the dumb thing was that I shouldn't be feeling this way. I had a family who loved me and an amazing best friend.

Trying to thrive in a guy-dominated field didn't help. Not when guys like Todd reminded me I didn't belong. My dad and I were close, but there was no way I was going to worry him about anything. He'd gone through so much when we lost Mama. The same with my brothers. I knew they'd swoop in if I asked for help, but we'd all been so lost after her death. Now that my brothers were each finding their way, I wouldn't worry them either.

But I'd had this growing feeling for the last few years now that I was lost. Sailing through life with no rudder to steer my ship. And I wasn't sure why. Some days I was confident in who I was. Other days I wished my mama had left me a map to navigate how to be a girl.

"So stop trying."

"What? Stop trying to be a mechanic?"

"No. Stop trying to fit in. Sometimes it's not about you. It's their problem."

Ha. Easier said than done. Especially if you hadn't experienced it.

"Have you ever felt like you never fit in?"

"Actually, I have. I know the feeling," he said, staring off into space before turning his dark gaze on me. "I'm adopted. My younger brother and I went into the foster care system before I turned three. My brother got adopted within the first month. The case worker said infants always get adopted first. All I knew was I wanted to go with him so badly. I couldn't figure out why his new parents didn't want me too."

That must have been so hard for a three-year-old to understand. My mind filled with the image of a small boy with big brown eyes filling with confusion and tears as his brother was taken away. Taken away by a family he'd hoped for. My heart hurt for both Grant the little boy and Grant the guy sitting next to me.

"I moved around the foster system for three years, each move brought new hope that it would be the last one. That someone would finally want me. That each new foster family would want to keep me. But for three years no one did. So, yeah, I know what not fitting in feels like."

"Grant... I'm so sorry. And now I feel completely ridiculous for complaining."

"Don't feel ridiculous. I only told you my story to show you that I get it. I understand what you're feeling." He shook his head with a grin. "And my story has a happy ending. Of course, now with hindsight, I can say the reason it took three years for me to be adopted was that I was waiting for the perfect parents to arrive. Sometimes when things seem dark it's because the shining light we're looking for is just around the corner where we can't see it."

"What happened to your brother? Do you get to see him?"

Grant's smile disappeared and his gaze moved away. "With closed adoptions, it took a few years to track him down. My dad had to file paperwork with the adoption agency to reach out to his family. I finally got to see him two years ago."

"And?"

"Let's just say it wasn't the reunion I'd hoped for." His gaze moved back to mine. He shrugged and shot me a smile that had my stomach fluttering. "So we're just a couple of misfits, I guess. Maybe it's just me—but I feel like we fit together."

"We fit together?" Warmth spread through my belly.

"Uh huh. You and me. I like you. Bernadette Jewell, would you like to go out with me?"

"Out?"

"Yes, on a date." He grinned. "I know. I'm totally springing this on you. A decent guy would have at least dropped a hint or two."

"Ha!" Grant had given me plenty of hints. I just hadn't believed him. "I told you... Teens don't date anymore."

He tilted his head and sent me a heated gaze that had my pulse revving up like it kicked into fourth gear. "Isn't that the beauty of not fitting in? We don't care what other teens do. We can do whatever we want, right?"

"Right. And you really want to take me on a date?" No guy had ever asked me on a date. I'd been asked to join pick-up games when they were short a player. I'd been asked to hang out. I'd been invited to watch the College Lacrosse Championships with some players on the varsity lacrosse team. I'd even been asked my opinion on girl issues, but those questions always started with "Hey, Bernie, if you were a girl..."

"More than I've wanted anything in a long time," he said, kicking my pulse into overdrive. "Guys on the team seem to like Burger Barn."

"They've got great burgers and excellent shakes."

"Excellent. So...is that a yes? You and me on a date to Burger Barn tomorrow night?"

"I'd like that," I said. Even as the words left my mouth, they didn't seem real. Was this my life? Was this me about to go out with an adorable, sweet nerdy guy? My cheeks were on fire.

"I say we change the subject before you change your mind. What's under the tarp?" Grant asked, making my gaze jerk over to the third stall in the garage. "Another project car?"

"Sort of." I sucked in a breath and let it out slowly. "It's my mom's old car. A Mustang."

"A Shelby?" His voice full of the proper awe a Shelby brings to real car enthusiasts.

"No." A Shelby would have been out of my mama's price range even back when she bought it.

"Can I look?"

"Um, sure." I stood, moving toward my mama's car, pulled in like a magnet. My muscles tensed as Grant drew the tarp off. I hadn't looked at the car in a very long time. Three years, in fact.

"A '68 convertible. Very sweet. I guess she doesn't drive it." His gaze ran over the car. "Is your dad restoring it for her?"

"He was. My mom died when I was eight."

Grant's head whipped around to me. "I'm sorry. That...sucks."

"Yeah. This was the first car my mama ever bought. She paid for it with her first job as a bank teller. It was her pride and joy. Her baby. Only, they had to sell it when my second brother arrived. When Mama got sick, Dad tracked it down and bought it back. It was trashed. The restoration gave them something to look forward to during the chemo treatments." I folded an arm over my stomach, squeezing tight. "He used to work on it while Mama sat in a chair next to him. When she got too sick to sit with him, he'd only work on it late at night after she was asleep."

On the nights when I woke up scared, I'd look out and see the light in the garage and fall back asleep knowing he was close by.

"And then...he stopped working on it so he could spend every minute at Mama's bedside." I remember being confused and sad watching him. I was too young to understand that my mama wasn't going to make it. Too young to know I should memorize her every word to me so I'd have them to keep forever. "And then she was gone and everything changed."

"I'm sorry, Bernie. So sorry." Grant eliminated the space between us. He wrapped his arms around me, pulling me into his chest.

The feeling of comfort shocked me. Along with the sting at the back of my eye sockets. I struggled to swallow down my urge to bawl my eyes out. For so long, I'd had this gaping hole in my heart. Not wanting to add to the burden my dad, brothers, and grandmas carried. But standing wrapped in Grants arms, the big gaping hole in my heart felt a bit smaller. Maybe the two of us did fit together.

15

POLKA MUSIC & CHEESY TOTS FOR THE WIN!

Grant

Here's the truth: I had travelled the world. Performed in front of huge crowds. Auditioned for big-name directors. Met famous celebrities and Presidents and even Kings and Queens.

But I stood on Bernie's porch more nervous than any of those other events. More nervous than waiting to hear if I'd won an Emmy or an Oscar.

"Come on in, Grant," Lolli said, pushing the screen door open. "Bernie should be right down."

I entered and stood in the foyer with Grandma Lolli while voices hissed upstairs.

Lacey, no. I'm not wearing a bow in my hair.

Fine, then what about this headband?

No. And not that shirt either.

So you're wearing a T-shirt and jeans? You should look special for a first date. Tell me how you look different than any other day at school right now.

What? Why would a boy ask me out and expect something differ-ent? But if you insist, instead of my serious face, I'll smile. How's that?

I grinned across at a wide-eyed Lolli and hollered up the

stairs, "That sounds more than fine to me!"

Part of what I liked about Bernie was she didn't put on any act. She didn't play coy, or dumb, or fake and flirty. I didn't want Bernie to be anyone else but who she was.

Bernie and Lacey came downstairs and sure enough—the sweet, slightly nervous smile on Bernie's lips and in her eyes was more than enough.

"Here she is." Lolli glanced at Bernie with a soft smile on her face. "Y'all have fun tonight."

"Yes, ma'am."

Lolli left the foyer for the back of the house and Lacey pushed both Bernie and me out the front door.

"Seriously, have fun. Although… I should tell you I made the mistake of mentioning that you two were going to Burger Barn to Grady…"

"Oh," I said.

"Oh what? Why is that bad?"

"Because Grady will probably show up just to give me a hard time."

"Lacey and I will protect you."

"Works for me. So, we'll see you later, Lacey." I opened the passenger door for Bernie who slid in while giving me the side-eye. Was she not used to nice guys?

"Sorry. Blame my mom." I shrugged, shut the door and walked around to slide in behind the steering wheel. After buckling in, I backed out of Bernie's driveway and headed into town. "As my date, you're entitled to change the radio station."

"You've got it on the Motown station; I'm good."

"Nice." I sent her a smile. "I guess it makes sense what with being named Bernadette, you grew up on classic Motown too."

"Yep. Also classic rock from my Dad. But, I also listened to all the popular polka hits, thanks to my grandma Gigi."

"Polka hits? I had no idea."

"Oh, yeah. You don't know what you missed." She reached

out, turning the dial on the station until—unbelievably—she tuned in a real live polka station. "Unless you've danced to "Polka! Polka! Polka!" on the kitchen floor, you really haven't lived."

Devil's Lap, Texas was a small town, so although Bernie lived on the outskirts where the older neighborhoods were, it was still only a ten-minute drive to Burger Barn in the original downtown.

The place was packed.

"Is it always this busy?" I leaned down so Bernie could hear me just as she turned to me and we stood face-to-face and lip-to-lip. "Bernie, I really want to kiss you right now—but I don't want to cheapen our first kiss."

Bernie blinked up at me with her crazy beautiful hazel eyes —looking more green than brown right now—and everything fell away. The people, the noise, the sawdust covered floors and the rustic decor all disappeared. It was just us. Me and Bernie and no-one else.

To my surprise, Bernie stood on her tiptoes and touched her lips to mine. It was soft and sweet and over before I could react.

Because Bernie pulled back and bit her bottom lip as her cheeks flushed a soft pink.

"Sorry. I-I knew I'd just be thinking about it through our whole meal once you mentioned it. So…I hope you don't mind. It didn't feel cheap—at all."

"Not at all." I brushed a loose curl off her cheek. "Now *I'll* be thinking about that kiss through our whole meal. But I'm not complaining. I'm also not counting that as our first official kiss. It's a fact that a first kiss has to be more than two seconds to be official."

"A fact, huh? I had no idea." Bernie's lips wobbled, fighting a smile as she turned to gaze up at the menu above the counter.

"Maybe even more like a rule. Who are we to thumb our noses at rules? I'm a nerd and embrace rules whole-heartedly." I turned to the menu, looking it over with interest. "Are the chocolate malt milkshakes any good?'

"All their shakes are good," Bernie said just as it was our turn at the counter.

"Welcome to Burger Barn. I'm Cashier Carl and I'm here to take your order." Some dude looking less than thrilled with having to work on a Saturday night asked while his eyes checked out some girls over at the drink machine. "What do you want in your feed bag?"

Feed bag? Guess they had a ranching theme going on.

"I'll take a bacon cheeseburger and a banana milkshake." Bernie looked at me.

"Can I try your shake?" I arched an eyebrow at Bernie who smiled and said yes. "Okay, then I'll take a chocolate malt shake, two cheeseburgers and an order of cheesy tots. Are they any good?"

The guy shrugged. "What's not to love about melted cheese on tots?"

"Good point. So, yes. An order of cheesy tots."

"That'll be twenty-three dollars and eighteen cents." Carl narrowed his eyes at me when I didn't immediately whip out my wallet. "You paying with cash or a card?"

That was the moment I realized I hadn't thought this through. I'd totally forgotten about paying for the date. As Kingsly Grant, I actually hadn't paid for anything in a few years. Not in person. Ever since my career took off four years ago, I'd been working nonstop. My assistant and my accountant handled all my bills.

"I forgot about paying. I don't have any cash or credit card on me." I was disappointed I'd overlooked something so basic. Something a regular guy would have thought of. Maybe even saved up his money to take his girl out. The dude behind the counter gave me a judgy look and sighed like I was the worst. Which, he had a point. "I'll have to—"

"I've got it," Bernie said, pulling some cash from her back pocket and handing it to the guy, now rolling his eyes at me. "As long as you're sharing the cheesy tots."

"I was sharing even when I thought I was paying." I wrapped an arm around her shoulders and drew her off to the side so others could order while we waited for my new best friend, Cashier Carl, to make our shakes. "And I don't share my food with just anyone."

"Bernard?" Todd Black's voice was as annoying as it was unwelcome, busting into our Saturday night. "Don't tell me. Let me guess… Y'all are on a study break. Because not even a nerd-nozzle like St-St-Stutterfield would date a guy like you, Bernard."

I turned to respond, but Bernie grabbed my hand and squeezed it lightly. Heck yes, I'd rather focus on Bernie holding my hand than Todd and his small-minded insults. I pulled her in closer and it was only then I heard her mumbling to herself. *Don't lose the bet. Don't punch him in the face. He's not worth it.*

Huh.

Sadly, Todd wasn't deterred and walked around to stand in front of us, wearing an idiot grin on his face.

"No answer for me, Jewell?" he prodded. "Tick tock, Bernard. Time's ticking. I hope you and Stutter-nerd are studying like crazy for the competition. Don't think I'm going easy on you just because you're a girl."

Punching Todd in the face did sound like a good idea. Which my lawyer would hate. Trust me on this.

Now, I hadn't taken Cashier Carl for a hero, but it just goes to reinforce that anyone can be heroic. Because Carl saved one of us from punching Todd in the face by calling out our number just then. Saved by the cheesy tots. We pushed around Todd, accepted the tray of food from Superhero Carl and found an empty booth to slide into.

We ate and I attempted to take Bernie's mind off of Todd by

telling her a funny story of when I learned to ride a two-wheeler. Only I changed the location from the Hollywood set of my first movie to Maple Street. And I changed the guy I accidentally hit from George Clooney to Uncle George. It was still funny enough to make Bernie laugh.

"Hey, you're late."

What? I looked up to find Grady and Lacey standing next to our booth.

"Late for what?" There was no way I'd have made a commitment during my date with Bernie.

"The thing," Grady said, frowning down at me. "And I found your missing hat. Here. Put it on."

He shoved the ball cap low on my head so I had to tilt my head back to peer up at him.

"It's not my—"

That was the moment I noticed the commotion a few tables away. One of the paparazzi with a notepad asking students if they'd seen King around town. Those darn tabloid rumors were building momentum.

"My favorite hat." I pulled the brim of the cap low over my eyes. "Thanks, man."

"Anytime. Now let's go do that thing." Grady used his body as a blocker. "Before it's too late."

"What thing?" Lacey asked, her forehead wrinkled with confusion. "Is this some guy thing?"

"Exactly," I mumbled. "A dude thing. Secret bro code stuff. Ready, Bernie?" I slid from the booth, pausing for Bernie to stand, letting her go in front of me. At the last second, I grabbed the paper boat of cheesy tots because hey—cheesy tots—and we made our escape.

Once out in the parking lot, I nodded my thanks to Grady for the save. See? I told you heroes were everywhere.

"Got your back, Stutterfield," Grady said. "Catch you later."

"Wait, what?" Lacey asked, hands on her hips. "You can't

leave us hanging. What's 'the thing' that was so important we had to rush over here. I'm dying to know what 'the thing' is."

"The thing?" Grady stood looking at a loss for words. "Right…the thing, Grant. Let's do the…thing. You go first."

"Absolutely." I handed my tots to Bernie and erased the space between me and Grady and gave him the biggest bro-hug I had in me. I'm not sure who was more surprised: Lacey, Bernie or Grady. Grady recovered quickly and hugged me back, stifling a laugh until we broke apart, serious again. "There you go. The thing. Now Bernie and I are heading out to finish our date."

Lacey narrowed her eyes at Grady while Bernie stood, head tilted, looking between the two of us. Then she shrugged and popped a tot into her mouth. My girl was cool as a cucumber, but I needed to wrap this up if I wanted any more cheesy tots.

Which Bernie knew. The girl was eating them one-at-a-time while she looked at me with a light of challenge in her eyes.

"Later, guys." I took Bernie's hand and led her away toward my car.

"Got you moving with the tots, didn't I?" Bernie snickered.

"A little with the tots. Mostly, I'm thinking about our official first kiss."

"*Eeep!*" she squeaked. "The 'official' part makes me nervous. What if we don't get it right?"

I took the opportunity to snag the tots back while she was flustered about the idea of our kiss.

Our kiss. Suddenly, *I* was flustered.

"Okay, I see your point. If it makes you feel better, this will be my first real kiss too. So, yeah, there's a bit of pressure to get it right. I mean, I don't want to mess it up to the point that you don't want to repeat it."

Sure, at eighteen, I'd kissed a few girls. Heck, my first ever kiss was on national TV when I was ten. And then with Talia in our movie together two years ago. That one *really* didn't count because the second our lips touched, it was clear we were just friends. All the other kisses were written into scripts. This would be my first *real* kiss too. The first kiss that meant something. The first kiss with a girl who made me forget my own name half the time.

I wasn't going to let our first real kiss be in the parking lot of Burger Barn. Not when I hoped this would be a story we'd tell years from now. I tossed the tots in the trash (now you know how serious I was about Bernie) and hustled her to my car and left the parking lot.

Deciding Bernie's front porch would be the perfect setting, I drove carefully toward her house.

"So, I'm liking this polka music," I said, attempting to distract us both from the growing tension over this all-important first kiss. Why did I have to open my mouth and make such a big deal over it? "I mean, it's not Motown, and not classic rock, and not old school country, and not Mozart, and not—"

"Pull over," Bernie said.

"What?" I jerked my head around to her, pulling over abruptly. "Are you sick? Are you okay?"

"Yes. I'm just—" She leaned into me and kissed me. Like really kissed me.

I went with it. I wrapped my hands around her face, threading the fingers of one hand into her crazy curls and kissed her back. Her lips were soft and she tasted sweet and my heart pounded so loudly in my ears, it darn near drowned out the polka music.

Our lips parted when we needed to come up for air. We sat, foreheads together, happily breathless.

"I'm sorry," Bernie said. "I couldn't take the stress. And that was more than two seconds, so it's official. You can't take it back."

"Take it back? Never in a million years." I kissed her forehead, gave her a long look, and focused ahead, pulling back onto the road. "It was perfect."

16

"ADORABLE" IS NOT IN THE TOMBOY CODE OF CONDUCT

Bernie

"Yes. This one works. It totally works, Lace." I stood staring at the girl in the orange evening gown wondering what in the heck would have made her put that monstrosity on.

"Hmmm, I'm not feeling it." Lacey stood behind me, looking into the full-length mirror at my reflection. "I don't think orange is your color."

"Are you sure?" It was pretty clear. The orange made me look like I was on day five of a one-week flu. I jerked my eyes away from the mirror and over to the pile of dresses sitting like a chiffon rainbow of Lacey's rejects. "You've sort of eliminated every other color and style. If I smile, maybe I'll look like a happy pumpkin."

"That's not a good thing." Lacey ran her gaze over the pile again with eagle eyes. "Oh, wait! Here's one I think we missed. What do you think?"

She'd pulled out a dress and was holding it up against her.

"I love it. Let's go with it."

"Good try, but go put it on." Lacey rolled her eyes and

shoved the dress in my hands, pushing me into the bathroom. "Let me see it before you take it off."

"This is the one." I let the orange dress fall to my feet as I shoved my arms and head inside the newest option, wiggling it on down. "I have a strong feeling about this one."

"Ha! You've said that every time."

I had. Was it wrong to want to make short work of this painful process? I'd already been trying on dresses for over thirty minutes which was thirty minutes over my limit. I was doing this because Lolli insisted, so to my mind, since I was only going to wear this dress for a total of ten minutes, it didn't really matter what it looked like.

"How's it look?" Lacey called from the other side of the door.

"It looks…" Like all the others? Too full of bows and ruffles? Too girly? Too everything? All true. But the color was nice. It reminded me of the original color of my mama's Mustang from photos I'd seen. Before the guy who'd bought it from her had let it sit in the sun for ten years: Tahoe Turquoise. "Hang on to your hat—and I'm not just saying this so we can be done, even though I've done that with every dress so far—but I think this one works."

I exited the bathroom for Lacey to see it.

"Oh my gosh! It's the perfect color for you." Lacey clapped and walked a whole circle around me, looking at the dress from every angle. "It looks great with your hair and brings out the green in your eyes. I don't love the bows, but—"

"But it works, right? I have a dress. Thanks, Lace." I hustled back into the bathroom to change into my old cutoff jean shorts and my Al's Garage T-shirt. I snagged a thick pair of socks and sat on my bed to lace up my work boots.

"Do you want to move on to makeup next?" Lacey asked just as my phone sounded with an incoming text on the bed behind me.

I twisted around to grab it and check. "It breaks my heart to tell you this, but I can't right now. That was Grant. He just got here and he's waiting for me in the garage."

"Is it going to be weird working with him now that you've kissed him?" Lacey asked.

"*Aaargh!*" I whipped my head around to her and stared. "Why did you say that? I should never have told you about the kiss, dang it. Of course it's going to be weird. But I didn't think about it until just now when you brought it up. Ugh. I've never worked on a car with somebody I've kissed before. What am I going to do?"

Lacey snickered. "I'm sure you'll figure it out."

Together, Lacey and I gathered up the rejected gowns to carry downstairs. We'd just reached the foyer when Lolli called from the kitchen.

"Did you find a gown?"

"Got the gown!" I called back.

"The color is gorgeous on her, Lolli! You'll love it!" Lacey added.

"Wonderful. Take the accordion to the garage so you can practice during your breaks!" she called again. "And tell Grant hello."

"Will do!" I pushed my back against the screen door since my arms were full of dresses, holding it open for Lacey. "It's a mystery to me why Lolli loves pageants so much."

"Maybe it brings her happy memories from when she was crowned Miss Armadillo." Lacey popped her trunk so we could lay the dresses inside. "Kiss Grant hello for me."

"Haha. That's not funny." I made a face at her. "You know I'm going to blush the minute I see him now."

"I know. You're adorable when you blush."

"No, I'm not. I'm never adorable." I scrunched my face at her and popped the trunk on my car to grab out the accordion. "Tomboys are not adorable. It's part of our tomboy code of conduct."

"Tomboys are totally adorable." Lacey got into her car, rolling the window down to add, "It's just you don't *think* you're adorable. You are."

"I'm going to pretend you didn't say that." I hefted the accordion strap over one shoulder and threw a wave in the air to her. "Later, Lace. Thanks for your help."

"Honestly, I'm having so much fun. And tomorrow we're doing makeup, so yay!"

She drove off and I headed to the garage realizing tomorrow —after the makeup session with Lacey—I'd have officially lost the make-over bet. I'd have to sell a few more lamps to pay all my brothers. And Gigi. Thank goodness Lolli and my dad didn't join the betting pool.

"Hey." Grant sent me a wide lopsided smile that magically made everything negative fly from my mind. "How's pageant practice going?"

"Found a dress, so both Lolli and Lacey are happy." I set the accordion onto the loveseat. "The bad news for you is that Lolli wants me to practice my talent on our breaks."

"How is that bad news?" Grant handed me our lacrosse sticks before grabbing his goalie equipment and the bag of balls and we walked around to the net on the side of the garage.

"You're either very nice, very optimistic or weirdly into painfully bad renditions of classic Beach Boy songs."

"Maybe I'm all three." He grinned at me and shoved on his helmet. "Or...maybe I like you so much that I'm willing to let you fire wicked-fast lacrosse balls at me, kill my enthusiasm for music and emasculate me with your encyclopedic car knowledge."

"Ha! Very funny." I dumped the bag of balls in the grass and scooped one up in my stick.

"I'm totally serious," he said.

"*What?*" I was in the process of taking a shot on the goal, but that threw me off and my hands jerked in the middle of my throw making it go wide by twenty feet. "You make me sound scary."

"If by scary you mean totally hot—then yes!"

I had no idea what to say to that. At all. So I stood there while my cheeks went hot.

"I'd say you're adorable when you blush, but I've been told women don't like that." He shrugged. "Besides, it isn't true."

"Not true? Lacey assured me I was adorable when I blushed."

"Lacey's wrong. You're not adorable when you blush."

"Not adorable?" Sure, I wore my brothers' hand-me-downs, had grease under my nails instead of pretty polish and the closest I got to perfume was eau-de-gasoline or when I detailed my car—but still... "Huh. Not even a little adorable?"

"Nope. Afraid not." He grinned at my frown and then he shook his head and hit me with his intense look. "You're beautiful."

"You're crazy," I said, ignoring the fact that my cheeks had moved from flushed to burning like the surface of the sun.

"Crazy for you. Now, let's finish this because I have a surprise for you."

"I don't do well with surprises." Ever since Mama got sick— and even more after she died—I found comfort in routine. An orderly predictable existence. Things I could count on.

"What if I tell you it's only a little surprise and I think you'll like it. Your grandma Lolli is helping me with it." He jumped up and snagged my shot. "What's your favorite color?"

"Tahoe Turquoise."

Grant had come up with a game to motivate each other. Each time Grant blocked a shot, he got to ask me a question. And each time I scored a goal past him, I got to ask *him* a question.

"That's weirdly specific," he said, arching an eyebrow at me.

"It's the original color of my mama's car and pretty close to the color of the pageant dress."

"Ah. That makes perfect sense now. And turquoise will bring out the green in your eyes."

"That's what Lacey said. How do people know these things?" I whipped off a shot to the upper corner of the goal which he missed. "Give me the three 'C's' of car repair."

"Concern: what the customer is complaining about. Cause: diagnose the vehicle to find out what's wrong. Correction: what repair and what parts are needed."

I took more shots on goal, making sure to hit his weak side. After we'd been practicing for thirty minutes, it was time to wrap it up. "Okay, last one for the night."

I wound up my shot, aiming for the upper corner of the goal on his weak side.

Grant took his goalie stance and proceeded to heckle me with "Swing, batter, batter, swing."

"Weak sauce, Stutterfield. First, that's the wrong sport. Second, that doesn't work on me. I grew up with four older brothers."

But just as I whipped off my shot, he winked. *He winked!* Apparently, winks did work on me since it distracted me enough to throw off my aim and Grant snagged the ball from the air before it hit the net.

"Ha! Who's the king of the goal?" He raised both gloved-hands high in the air, waving his goalie stick in victory after a sweet save. "What's your favorite movie?"

"I don't have one."

"What? That's impossible." He pulled off his helmet and gloves, tossing them all into his equipment bag. "Favorite TV show?"

"Nada."

"Bernadette Jewell, that's un-American. Do you know how many hours of television the average American teen watches?" He ran his hands through his damp hair, yet somehow the curls all fell into a sexy disarray. "Over twenty-two hours a week! The government, the Nielsen Ratings Company and I want to know what you're doing with your twenty-two hours."

"Um…living? I don't know. I work at Al's, work on cars, play sports and just stay busy." I shrugged. "I never could sit still long enough to watch a whole show."

"I'm going to let you get away with that answer because it's a good one." He pointed at me. "But it's also time for the surprise. Wait here…"

EXACTLY LIKE A HERO

Bernie

I watched him jog off to my front porch and into my house. It had taken Grant all of five minutes to charm Lolli. The guy didn't seem to have a shy bone in his body. He did everything with confidence—even the stuff he was bad at like lacrosse and cars. It was like his curiosity outweighed his ego.

Grant returned with a quilt tucked under one arm and Lolli's picnic basket in the other.

"What are you doing?"

"Solving a problem." He grinned at me. "See, we're short on time, right?"

"Yes." We were making good progress but the clock was definitely ticking when it came to the auto tech state finals.

"And it's time for our second date..." He handed me the quilt and picnic basket. "Hold these, please."

"Our second date?" I asked, watching him go into the garage and come back out with the old folding table dad used to use when he tail-gated before my brothers' football games. He set it up under the oak tree shading the garage, covered it with the quilt only to disappear back into the garage and return with the portable work light that had been hanging from Earl's hood.

"Absolutely our second date." He swung the cord of the work light over one of the lower tree branches so that it hung, swaying softly over our heads and the table. "Where could we go for a second date that wouldn't take much time and would keep us from running into Todd again?"

Not that I had to be sold to agree to a second date, but he totally sold me on not running into Todd.

Grant disappeared back into the garage and must have plugged in the extension cord for the light because it lit up. He came back out carrying our wheeled work stools, setting them at the table.

"Bernie, would you like to go on a picnic with me?" He held out his hand for mine.

"I'd love to." I took his hand and he helped settle me onto a stool.

"I'll admit the light is overkill since it's still light out." Grant sat and dug into the picnic basket, pulling out paper plates, napkins and serving up Lolli's fried chicken, pasta salad and biscuits. "But who doesn't want a little romantic ambiance on a second date, right?"

"I'm not complaining." At all. It turned out, even a tomboy like me liked romance—especially when it was a guy as nice, cute and funny as Grant.

Our second date was a success. We ate and talked and laughed.

"Time's up." Grant wiped his mouth on one of Lolli's fabric napkins and cleared our picnic remnants back into the basket. "Back to work. I for one won't be happy unless I know we've done everything in our power to beat Todd."

"You and me both," I agreed.

We worked under Earl and over at the workbench for the next two hours. As we worked, I quizzed Grant on all things tires, four-stroke engines, safety standards and circuit boards. We focused on the stations in the morning session that required individual responses. The afternoon was all team work. I'd take the lead on diagnosing & repairs while Grant backed me up with his knowledge, being our parts-runner and double-checking to make sure our ROs were filled out correctly. We had a solid plan of attack.

The only thing Grant had trouble picking up was when I taught him how to solder a wire harness.

"Ouch!" Grant dropped the soldering iron onto the table, shaking his hand in pain. "Dang it, that's the second time I've burned myself."

"Sorry. There is a learning curve." I grabbed his hand and guided him over to the sink where I slid his hand under running water. "If it makes you feel any better, I did the same thing while I was learning."

"Not right at this moment it doesn't." He gave me a lopsided grin. "Besides, you were probably ten when you learned to solder."

"Actually, I was six." I handed Grant an ice pack from the top freezer before grabbing us water from the fridge and then sprawled on the loveseat. "Dad decided to teach me how after he caught me messing with his."

"Smart dad." Grant nudged me over so he could sit down next to me. "Do you think he'll finish restoring the Mustang?"

"No." My gaze moved to the car in question, once again covered by the tarp. "It's been sitting under that tarp since my mama died. Dad gave it to me the day I turned fifteen."

I felt Grant's head whip around to me.

"The Mustang is yours?"

"She is." Like it always happened whenever I thought about the Mustang—my lungs felt like they were being squeezed by some giant invisible hand. "Tammi is all mine."

"Tammi?"

"Mama named her car after Tammi Terrell."

"Right. How could I forget your mom's love of Motown? 'Ain't No Mountain High Enough,' 'If I Could Build My Whole World Around You,' 'Ain't Nothing Like the Real Thing.'"

Huh. Obviously, he was familiar with Tammi & Marvin's greatest hits.

"So why haven't you started restoring the Mustang?"

"I don't know." I knew. I shrugged, ignoring the way my stomach twisted whenever I thought about working on Tammi. I just…couldn't yet. The only way I'd made it this far was with strict control of both my life and my emotions. I couldn't think about my mama and her car—not without feeling like I'd explode into a million little pieces that might never go back together. "Time and money for parts I guess."

"Uh huh. So that shelf of Mustang parts is for…?"

"Has anyone told you that you're hyper-observant to the point of being annoying?" I asked, frowning across at him.

"A few times as a matter of fact." He grinned, but took my hand in his, giving it a comforting squeeze. "I'm just trying to understand. I feel this burning need to understand everything about you and what's going on inside that head of yours."

I sucked in a huge breath of air. "When my dad gave me Mama's car, he gave me his restoration plans. So I have a list of all the parts I need. Ever since I've had the car…whenever I have this overwhelming need to scream and cry about my mama…I shut it down and buy a part from the list. One day—when looking at the car doesn't make me feel empty inside—then I'll be ready to restore her."

Grant stood and walked over to the shelf of Mustang parts. He even flipped through the clipboard of paperwork hanging from a nail on the shelf, running his finger down the three-page parts list before running his gaze over all the parts.

"You've bought a lot of parts." He looked at me, his eyebrows pulled down low over narrowed eyes.

"I have." Each part on those shelves represented a time when the overwhelming loss of my mama threatened to pull me under. And it scared me, so I managed it the only way that made sense.

"Come here," he said, pulling me up and into his chest. "You're killing me, Bernadette. You're one of the strongest people I've known. But I wish I'd met you three years ago so you could have called me every time you felt like screaming or crying. I'd have come running."

"Like a hero," I half laughed, half cried into his chest.

"Exactly like a hero." He wrapped his arms even tighter around me and pressed his lips to my temple.

"Well, you're here now." I closed my eyes, relaxing against him. I wasn't used to sharing my sadness, but if it always felt this good, I could get used to it.

18

A LOSS & A WIN

Grant

Mom: *Alison just sent me an ALL CAPS text to check on you. She thinks you might be having a heart attack.*

I looked up from my mom's text, scanning the sidelines of the lacrosse field to see who was doing today's workout for me.

Josh—and he was doing it while polishing off a party pack of tacos from Taco Loco.

I laughed and texted my mom back.

Me: *Tell her I'm fine. Just doing a workout wearing a weighted vest.*

Maybe Alison would buy that excuse.

We'd just lost another lacrosse game—but a close one—and were doing cool downs and having a captain's meeting on the field.

"Good effort, guys. We played a solid game." Grady looked around at the team. "We kept it close thanks to Grant."

"Horse shit," some guy in the back mumbled.

"How many goals did you score, Chad?" TJ asked, his gaze laser focused on the dude. "How many passes did you intercept? How many guys did you run down?"

That shut Chad up.

"TJ is right. This is a team effort," Grady said. "It takes all of us to win a game and takes all of us to lose a game. So don't criticize a teammate unless you can say you played a perfect game."

I didn't let Chad bother me. Making movies was a team effort too. Even though I was a big enough star and could probably get away with throwing fits and blaming someone else if a scene wasn't working and we had to do a retake—I didn't. My parents made sure I knew that being famous didn't make me better than anyone else. I owned my mistakes and accepted when other people made them. That's what being a team meant. No one was more important than any other part of the team.

Besides, my practice with Bernie was paying off. Grady told me a good goalie stops about fifty percent of the shots on goal. Granted, I had a lot of room for improvement, but I'd say I'd gone from stopping ten percent of the shots on goal to over thirty percent. Not bad in a week.

My goal was to improve enough to actually help win a game. We *would* win a game before I left or I'd die trying.

"All right, let's bring it in," Dax DeLeon, the third captain, called. "Our next game is on Friday. We're prime for a win, so let's practice hard the rest of this week."

"Sticks in," Grady said and we all moved in, putting the heads of our sticks into the circle. "Jackalopes on one."

"*Jackalopes!*" we chorused and then broke apart.

"*Grant!*"

I turned to the bleachers, searching the stands, and sure enough there was my dad standing next to Mom. I waved and jogged over, meeting them on the track that separated the bleachers from the field.

"You made it!" I hugged my dad before moving to give Mom a one-armed hug. "Well, what did you think?"

"My first thought was when the heck did you learn to play lacrosse?" Dad said. "My second thought was how cool it was that our son plays varsity lacrosse." I will always remember the look of excitement on my dad's face in this moment. He loved sports, so this was his moment to finally, finally get to be the proud sports-nut dad. "My third thought was you're a little weak on your left side."

"I know, I know. That's what Bernie's been telling me." I laughed and turned to search the crowd for Bernie. She was standing next to Lacey, but looking my way so I motioned her over. "I want you to meet Bernie."

"I'd love to meet all your teammates." Dad's gaze scoured the field for this "Bernie" dude.

Bernie slid in next to me looking unsure.

"Mom. Dad. I'd like you to meet Bernie." I wrapped my arm around her waist and drew her up next to me. "Bernie, these are my parents, April and Brock Gr...uh-Stutterfield."

"It's nice to meet you, Bernie." Dad shook her hand.

Mom, on the other hand, threw her arms around Bernie and gave her a big hug. "I feel like I already know you. Grant's been filling me in on everything."

"E-everything?" Bernie pulled back, looking alarmed. "I'm not sure—"

"Everything about you helping me with lacrosse and me helping you with the auto shop competition." I squeezed her waist gently.

"Oh, sure." Bernie smiled at my parents. "Your son is a sponge with information. And, surprisingly, under his nerd exterior is a great athlete."

"That sounds like our Grant."

"Hey, some of the team is even patting me on the butt after a save, so I must be getting good," I bragged.

"Then I'm looking forward to the next game," my dad said. And I knew he was, no matter whether we won or lost. But, man, did I want to win. For both of us.

＊ ＊ ＊

The rest of the week, Bernie and I went full throttle on studying and lax practice. I had a lacrosse game on Friday night and the Texas High School Automotive Technology Competition was on Saturday. We stayed up late with Motown music in the background keeping us moving and inspired. It felt like we'd taken everything to the next level.

The only thing not improving was Bernie's accordion skills. Sadly, no matter how hard she tried it always sounded like she was torturing a cat.

I played piano and guitar and sang, so maybe I could give her a tip to help.

"It might help to remember, melody on the right; bass on the left," I offered.

"What?" She squeezed the accordion together, making the bellows howl painfully. "I have no idea what that means!"

"Oh, okay. Then it sounds great!" I gave her two thumbs up. "Keep going!"

It was a good thing she wasn't trying to win the pageant. Accordion playing was not one of her talents. Which was why her not giving up was even more impressive. I admired that she took time to practice the talent for Lolli even though her priority was the auto competition. That said a lot about who Bernie was.

Before I knew it, it was game time on Friday night. My mom, dad, and Bernie were all in the stands to cheer us on. I had a rough first half. TJ stopped me before I ran on the field for the second half.

"You've got this, Grant. You're fearless in the net." He grabbed my facemask and looked me firmly in the eyes. "We'll score as many goals as we can and you stop as many as you can. Deal?"

"Deal." All I could say was that everything clicked into place in the second half. Everything my teammates had taught me, everything Bernie had coached me on, every one of her eye-hand coordination exercises and her gazillion shots on goal all came together.

I was the Karate Kid catching a fly with chopsticks. I was Phil Connors finally figuring out how to escape Groundhog Day. I was Harry Potter mastering his wand. You know what? Not to brag, but I even think I was Rocky beating Apollo Creed.

I saw every ball like it was in slow motion. I stepped with my lead foot. I was all over my weak side so much that I didn't *have* a weak side. I snagged balls from the air right and left. I made a few stellar saves that earned me pats on the butt, punches to my shoulder, and even a "You're the man, Stutterfield!" Grady was so pumped up after one of my saves that he hit his helmet against mine and told me he loved me.

We won the game 12-5.

Let me just say, winning felt as good as I thought it would.

"Dude, you really stepped up your game." Grady pointed at me and nodded. "Most of the team is going to the field party. You and Bernie should come."

"Can't." As much as I wanted to experience a field party, that wasn't going to happen tonight. Tomorrow was our big day. Bernie's big day. She was counting on me and I wasn't going to show up tired. This winning feeling that I had tonight, I wanted Bernie to have the same feeling tomorrow. "Maybe next time."

My parents and Bernie found me as the crowd thinned out. Dad wrapped me up in a big hug. He was so excited he even picked me up off the ground.

"You played a wonderful game, honey." Mom beamed at me. "You've improved so much since your first game! It was like watching a different player."

"That's all on account of Bernie." I realized I was already holding Bernie's hand. It happened automatically without a single thought. And it felt natural and necessary. "She's been coaching me for two weeks now."

"That was all you," Bernie said.

"I'm guessing it was both of you. It was also fun to watch," Dad said. "I'm glad I could get away from work to watch it. You're my boy, blue."

"Hahaha, Dad. How long have you been waiting for that quote?"

"He's been waiting forever," Mom said, rolling her eyes. "It's a little sad that this was your last game."

"Man, you're right." I can't believe I forgot that. The team had only needed me for three weeks. Rob had already started back to practice this week. And after tomorrow, my time in Texas was up. Not something I wanted to think about right now.

"Well, consider me a proud parent even if your high school athletic career as a starting goalie only lasted three weeks."

"Thanks, Dad. Bernie and I are heading back to her place to get a few more hours of studying in."

"Not too late," Mom said. "It'll be a long day for you both tomorrow."

After I showered and changed in the locker room, Bernie and I headed out, stopping off to grab a pizza to take back to her garage. We were done with hands-on training. So we sat inside Earl while we shared our pizza, reviewed a few highlight items and talked through our plan for tomorrow.

"I think we're ready," Bernie said, wiping her mouth and hands with her paper napkin before placing it into the empty pizza box.

I added my own napkin to the box before tossing it out the window.

"I just wanted to thank you again for doing this for me."

Bernie darted her eyes to mine and then away again. "You really went above and beyond with the amount of time and effort you gave to me. It means a lot."

"Hey, who wouldn't do that for their girlfriend?"

"Wh-what?" She looked at me with those big eyes of hers. "Your girlfriend?"

I didn't mean to say that. I shouldn't have said that. I knew I shouldn't have said that even though I meant it. Because mom was right when she said I needed to let Bernie know who I was before we took this any further. There was no way I could do that tonight—not the night before the competition. The competition which meant everything to her. That's why I should've kept my mouth shut. As soon as the competition was over, I would tell her.

"Do you know what? This was a dumb conversation for me to start considering what a big day we have tomorrow. So, pretend I didn't say anything about you being my girlfriend."

"Oh. Okay, um...sure." She turned her face away and looked out Earl's front windshield.

"Bernadette..." I reached out my hand, cupping her cheek to gently turn her face toward mine. "I've never met a girl like you. I like everything about you. I like that you're beautiful and don't even know it. I like that you're a better tech than the guys in shop class, but you never brag or put anyone else down. I like that you're confident and willing to put yourself out there and claim a spot in a man's world even when they try to crowd you out. I like how much you love your grandmothers even when they blackmail you. I like that you share your junk food with me. But I really, really love the way your eyes go from hazel to green and your pulse kicks up when I get close to you.

"I could keep going, but we have to get up early tomorrow morning. And of course, there's that other thing..."

"What other thing?" Her breath hitched.

"I really want to kiss you right now."

"Grant?" The pulse in her neck fluttered and her eyes shone like faceted emeralds.

"Yes?"

"Shut up and kiss me."

"You don't have to tell me twice." I closed the space between us, keeping one hand on her cheek and sliding my other hand around to her ponytail. I took it slow, pressing my lips against hers. My heart beat so hard I was sure she could hear it. Every muscle in my chest tightened.

She kissed me back, her soft lips pressing firm against mine and a jolt of intuition hit me again. In that moment, I knew we were meant to be together. Maybe just friends. Maybe more. It sure felt like more.

After one last press of my lips to hers, I pulled away to catch my breath and let Bernie catch hers.

"How about this? How about we focus on tomorrow, you know, beating the pants off of Todd, and then finish this discussion?"

"That sounds like a great plan. I'm in." She smiled up at me. "I'm all in."

19

LET'S DO THIS

Bernie

"Good morning students, sponsors, and proud family members! Welcome to the Texas High School Automotive Technology Competition! Teams... Go to your workstations!"

"We are so ready for this," I said to Grant as we strode to our first assigned station.

Both my grandmas and Grant's mom were all in the audience cheering us on. I felt cool and confident. So confident that not even Todd's condescending smirk from across the room got to me.

"Oh yeah. As Ricky Bobby says, let's shake and bake." Grant grinned and raised his hand, ready for a fist bump.

"I don't know who your friend Ricky Bobby is, but okay." I fist bumped him back as he laughed at me. "Let's do this."

The morning session consisted of three hours of workstations. Each team would rotate to six different workstations. Each station had a judge to administer a specific task. Not only did the three hours fly by, somehow Grant just made it more fun.

We sailed through engine mechanics, steering and suspension, and brakes. I took the lead on the technical issues, and Grant stepped in when it came to memorized charts and facts. Having a teammate with a photographic memory was awesome.

When it came to the job interview station, I may have been passionate about being a technician, but Grant took the interview to a whole new level. His answers were eloquent, prepared and his delivery smooth and engaging. The guy was a natural at this. Thanks to Grant, we aced the job interview workstation.

The few times I got tense, Grant gently squeezed the back of my neck to calm me down or he'd raise his hand for a high five to boost my confidence up. The guy was a rock.

We had an hour for lunch before the afternoon session, and they served us bag lunches in a large conference room while they played videos about career opportunities in the auto industry.

"Hey," Grant whispered, leaning his shoulder against mine. "I'm totally counting this as our third date."

"That works for me." I took a bite of the sub sandwich to hide my smile.

"Which means I get to pick where we go for our fourth date."

Our fourth date. Yeah, I liked the sound of that. My attention was caught by a loud discussion a few tables over. When I looked, unsurprisingly, it was Todd having heated words with his teammate, Steve.

"Either Todd can't take pressure," Grant said. "Or this morning didn't go well for him."

"I don't know. Todd's a good technician. Sometimes he's just a jerk for no reason."

The video ended and one of the judges announced the afternoon session was about to get underway.

We stood, dumped our trash on our way out and found our team's car out on the arena floor. Each team had an identical Ford vehicle with identical pre-staged problems under the hood. We had three hours to diagnose and repair as many problems as we could.

"This is going to be fun to watch," Grant said.

"Whoa. Watch? We're a team." I gave him a half-amused side eye. "We're doing this together."

"Absolutely, but you should see yourself when you get lost in a car's engine. You get this laser focus and your brain works through and eliminates the options at some speed light years ahead of me. It's impressive."

"Thanks." I narrowed my gaze on him. "For a minute there, I thought you were going to say I was adorable when I worked on cars."

"Heck, no. Would I say something like that? I believe we've already established that you are absolutely *not* adorable when you work on cars." He looked away from me but his lips tilted into a small smile. "You're beautiful. And hot."

The judges entered the room, took their places where they would monitor their assigned teams, and the "On-Car" Challenge of the competition began.

Rushing to our car, we lowered our protective goggles in place, threw open the hood and reached for the first repair order (RO) to read the short description of why the vehicle was "in for service." Together, we talked through the possibilities, ran some basic diagnostics and found our first fault. Grant grabbed the manual and looked up the code.

"Blown gasket." I carefully and quickly filled out the 3-Cs (Concern, Cause, Correction), making sure to put the correct part number we needed before handing it off to Grant.

While he ran it to the parts counter, I started working on the next RO. This one raised a red flag about the throttle position sensor, so I connected the digital volt ohm meter to check. Yep. The sensor was bad. I wrote up the RO for that—making sure to fill out the 3-Cs—and handed it off to Grant who had just come back with the gasket.

Grant and I worked smoothly together. Every time we finished repairing a problem, we high-fived and moved on to the next. We were moving at top speed but keeping safety rules in mind and focusing on our attention to detail.

I felt good by the time they called our last official bathroom break. Grant went off to grab us some water while I made a run for the bathroom. I had just flushed the toilet and was about to exit my stall when the door to the bathroom slammed open as someone else came in. The fact that the voices weren't female had me pausing in my stall.

"What's wrong with you?" A man's voice vibrated with anger. "You're losing to a girl! *A girl!* Are you trying to embarrass me? Or are you just stupid?"

"I'm trying." *Todd's voice.*

"Then you need to try harder. Can you imagine how it reflects on me? I taught you everything you know about cars. But my own kid can't beat a girl in a tech competition."

"She's good, Dad."

"You're better! *You. Will. Be. Better.* You will *not* lose to a girl. Do you hear me?" Todd's dad snorted his distain. "Oh, hell. Get those tears out of your eyes. Why can't you be like your brother? He went all the way to Nationals. You're a loser compared to him."

"I'm not a loser. No girl's going to beat me."

"You better pull it together, you worthless sack of shit."

What did I just hear? My hands shook and a knot twisted in the pit of my stomach. I'd never heard a parent talk to their kid like that. It was painful to listen to. I couldn't imagine living with that day in, day out.

I waited until I heard the door swoosh open and closed before exiting the stall. Only, Todd hadn't left. He stood, leaning on the sink near the door with his shoulders hunched and his head hanging like it was too heavy for his neck.

His head jerked up when the stall door squeaked and our eyes locked in the mirror.

He scrubbed one hand over his eyes, morphing from a boy in emotional pain to a puffed-up, sneering bully right before my eyes.

"What are you looking at?" he growled. "What are you doing in here?"

"Using the *girl's* bathroom." I stepped over to a sink, washing my hands quickly so I could get away from Todd and the echoing sound of his dad's ugly words.

"You didn't hear anything," he said, his voice tight, like when you try to hold back tears and it makes your whole throat hurt. "Don't look at me like that. I don't need or want your pity."

"I don't feel pity for you," I lied, avoiding his eyes as I rushed from the bathroom.

I was still shaking when I rejoined Grant at our car. My insides felt like I was stuck out in an ice storm when brittle cold air freezes your lungs until you think they'll crack.

We had less than an hour left in the competition but my thoughts were scattered. *Pull it together, Jewell. We only have one last problem to repair. Focus.* I had to read the repair order twice because I couldn't push the stark pain in Todd's eyes or his dad's voice telling him he was worthless from my head. *Worthless.* Who says that to their own child? To any child?

Maybe Todd needed this win more than I did. Sure, I needed the scholarship money, but I could work for a year and save up for tech school. I had a father who loved and supported me. Todd… didn't.

I wouldn't say I made a conscious decision to throw the contest. But a small voice inside me told me to loosen my grip… ease up… If I made a small mistake that created space for Todd to slide into first place it wouldn't be the end of my world.

It came down to want vs. need. I *wanted* the win to prove I was a good mechanic, but my dad and grandmas would love me no matter how I did in the competition.

From what I'd just heard in the bathroom, Todd needed the win more than I did.

What should I do? Give in to instincts and go with my gut? Or keep a cool head, stay strong, and keep my competitive edge?

What was the right thing to do? Todd definitely did *not* want my pity. If he found out, he'd probably hate it more than having his father yell at him. Maybe I should just stay out of it, do my best and let Todd handle his own life.

"Bernie, let's go. Are you with me?" Grant stood with his hand out waiting for me to do my part. "We're running out of time. Do you have the RO ready?"

20

WHAT HAPPENED IN THERE?

Bernie

"Yeah, hang on…" I bent my head down and wrote out the repair order only to be distracted even more by a growing buzz of conversation traveling through the arena like a groundswell. Looking around, more and more people were turning to stare at our team. Where had all the cameras and reporters come from? Were they taking our picture because I was the only girl in the competition this year?

Focus, Bernie. Biting my lip, I quickly finished writing out the repair order…giving one last look at the 3-Cs. No time to change it now.

I handed the RO to Grant who turned to rush to the parts counter, but paused mid-stride. Had he just noticed the photographers and attention too? Did everyone know we were in first place heading into this last hour?

Grant tugged his hat lower and disappeared through the frantic final dashes to the parts counter as the time ticked down. Grant and I were able to replace our last part just as the judge called time over the P.A. system.

"You okay?" Grant put his hand under my chin, guiding our gazes together. "It felt like I lost you there at the end."

"Yeah, I just—I don't know." Without even thinking, I stepped into him, burying my face against his shoulder. When he wrapped his arms around me everything felt better. Everything. "Can I just stay here inside your arms for the next few hours…days…maybe longer?"

"Absolutely," he said, but his arms and chest went tense.

Too much PDA? Or maybe he was finally giving into the tension of the day?

"Congratulations to all our students today. You're all winners in our book. But someone has to win the scholarship prizes, so if you'll turn your attention to the screen behind me, our computer has tabulated the results."

I didn't look. I couldn't.

Grant did.

"Huh. Todd came in second. We finished fourth." I felt more than saw Grant's look of confusion. Right. Because we'd been on fire the whole day. "I'm not sure how that happened…"

"Maybe the other teams finished strong," I said. "That last repair sort of stumped me, I guess."

"No. It was me. If I'd been a stronger partner, you wouldn't have had to carry such a heavy load during the day." He stroked his hand over my hair, comforting me. "Feels like a tougher loss, since we were leading for most of the competition. I thought we had it. Didn't you?"

Before I had a chance to come up with a response, the announcer got our attention again.

"I've got a special surprise. It's come to my attention we have a celebrity in the competition today. Ladies and gentlemen, please welcome movie star, Kingsly Grant, competing for Jackson High School! Thank you, Kingsly Grant, for helping to bring awareness to the field of auto tech!"

"Jackson?" There were only four students representing Jackson here today.

Journalists and paparazzi flowed toward us like an incoming tide, their cameras clicking away, taking photographs and yelling questions to Grant.

…Just like he was a movie star on the red carpet.

Grant? Grant, who had turned as stiff as a marble statue?

Oh no. *No, no, no, no.* Please don't let this be true. Grant—*my Grant*—was Kingsly Grant the movie star? No.

I tilted my head back to look up into Grant's face and I knew it was true.

The one boy I'd learned to trust had been lying to me the whole time.

"Bernie," he said, reaching for my hand as I pulled out of his arms and away.

"I told you I don't do well with surprises," I said, taking a step back from him…and then another.

"Bernie, we need to talk."

"We actually don't." I spun around, pushed my way through the crowd of students and rushed out the back entrance to the parking lot.

Guess who followed me.

"Bernadette, please stop. Talk to me." Grant snagged my hand at the edge of the parking lot, turning me to face him. "What happened in there?"

"What happened?" My voice shook. "Uh…everyone found out my teammate is Hollywood's biggest teen heartthrob who's been hiding in plain sight."

"I'm sorry. I was trying to find the right way to tell you. Then I realized it didn't matter."

"It didn't matter?" How could he think it didn't matter?

"Yes. Because you're not impressed with all the Hollywood stuff. You couldn't care less that I'm an actor."

"True. But I do care about being lied to. About you laughing behind my back."

"I never laughed at you."

"Sure you didn't. All that stuff about your first kiss." *Our first kiss.* I didn't think I could be more embarrassed. Or angry. If I were lucky, a black hole would appear right now and suck me up and away. "I'm an idiot. Was there anything about us that wasn't a lie?"

"That wasn't a lie. My first kiss was on a set for a TV show when I was ten. Back when I still thought girls had cooties. Of course, I didn't count that. My next kiss was on a movie set. I was sixteen and it was with my best friend; it was like kissing my sister."

"Whatever. The kisses are your smallest lie." Relief flowed through me when I saw Gigi's car approaching. "No wonder it was so easy for you to give that 'you don't need to fit in' advice. *You* don't need to fit in. You never have because you're loved by millions."

"It's a lonely way to go through life. Too young to fit in with most of the actors. Too famous for regular friends." He shrugged. "I've never had the chance to fit in somewhere. Not until now. With you."

"Too bad you didn't trust me enough to tell me."

"Trust works both ways."

"Whatever."

"Bernie—"

Grant's mom pulled up in her car and rolled the window down. "Grant, honey, you've been outed."

"I know."

"Hi, Bernie. I'm sorry about the competition."

"Thanks, Mrs. Stutterfield, I mean...is that really your name?" I whipped my head to Grant—*Kingsly.* "Is she even your mom?"

"Yes, she's my mom."

"Although, it's actually Mrs. Grant."

"I didn't lie to you about anything else." He held his hand to me. "Just that one thing."

"Right. That one huge thing that changes everything." I rolled my eyes, because nothing about him—about Grant Stutterfield—had been the truth.

"Grant, there's more paparazzi on the way. We need to go."

"Bernie, I really need to talk to you. To explain."

"What's to explain? It's pretty clear what happened." I looked at Grant, still hovering next to me. "You lied to me and pretended to be someone you're not. You should go."

"You still didn't answer me. What happened in there? We were winning going into the last round. I know we were. What the heck happened?"

"I messed up. It turns out I'm not as good of a mechanic as I thought I was."

"Now which one of us is lying?"

"Why do you even care?" Thankfully, Gigi pulled up to the curb just then behind Grant's mom because I needed to leave before I burst into tears.

I walked to Gigi's sedan, tearing the back door open as more cars pulled into the parking lot and tabloid reporters spilled from the building.

"Grant…" his mom called.

"We are not finished here," he said, giving me one hard look before getting into the car with his mom and driving off.

Proof that the famous Kingsly Grant wasn't perfect. Because he was wrong.

We were so finished.

21

A DEFINITE SPOON EMERGENCY

Bernie

So much for big plans. The original plan after the competition was for me and Grant to drive home together so we could stop and celebrate our win. Yeah, that's how confident we'd been. I never in a million years could have predicted how it actually went down.

The fact that we lost, while painful, wasn't the craziest or most painful part of the evening. Nope.

So now Grandma Gigi was driving us home with Grandma Lolli sitting next to her, throwing worried glances at me in the back seat. The Motown station was on the radio—probably to help make me feel better—but for the first time, it really wasn't.

Gigi reached out and turned the music down.

"So let's discuss the elephant in the car," Gigi said, her eyes meeting mine in the rear view mirror. "Your Grant is really Kingsly Grant, the movie star."

Yep. Grant Stutterfield was Kingsly Grant. I couldn't wrap my head around it.

"He's *not* my Grant." Not anymore. If he ever really was. It was all an act, right? Some publicity stunt for his movie?

"So you didn't know?" Lolli asked. "He didn't tell you who he was?"

"No. He failed to share that information with me."

Ugh. I tried to push him from my mind, but my brain kept flashing up moments of all the time we'd spent together. With each memory the more appalled—and angry—I got.

My first kiss ever? I wasn't mad that Grant Stutterfield was the first boy I kissed. I was mad that he'd told me I was his first real kiss, but there was no way I was *Kingsly Grant's* first kiss.

The fact that I "coached" Kingsly Grant—a guy known to be a great athlete who does half his own stunts according to Lacey —for two weeks! Was he laughing at me the whole time?

And the cars! All the pride I'd felt over my project car and our team car in shop class—and Kingsly Grant probably had a fleet of fancy high-priced cars in his garage.

"Did he—"

"Can we not talk about him right now please?" I knew my grandmas were simply trying to be there for me, but I just couldn't deal with Grant/King right now.

"Sure, but that leaves us with the competition," Gigi said.

Right. The great thing about my grandma Gigi was how she tackled things head on. That was also the not great thing about her in moments like this.

"What's to talk about? I lost. Again." I stared out the window at the blur of fenced pasture land and cows we passed.

"It's such a shame, too." Lolli sent me a soft smile. "You and Grant were in the lead after the morning session. I simply don't understand how you lost."

"It's a mystery, isn't it, Bernie?" The other great/non-great thing about Gigi was how perceptive she was. Did I mention my grandma Gigi used to be a police detective? Oh, yeah. Dad used to say Gigi made Walker Texas Ranger look like an amateur.

I knew if I went with an "I guess I'm not as good a tech as I thought I was" excuse, Gigi would pounce all over it.

Because that wasn't what happened. But considering I wasn't sure I understood why I did what I did, I had serious doubts that Gigi would like hearing the real explanation. Lolli might, but she had a marshmallow for a heart like Mama, so yeah.

"No, Gigi." I looked straight into her eyes in the rear-view mirror again. "It's not a mystery. But it is done and I do want to talk to you both about it—just not yet, okay?"

"Take all the time you need, dear," Lolli said.

"Just make sure all the time you need doesn't last more than forty-eight hours," Gigi said. "Sometimes it's better to deal with things sooner rather than letting them fester. That goes for the competition and Grant."

I wasn't planning on letting things fester. I was hoping I could bury it all deep, throw lime over it to help it decompose faster and pretend none of it ever happened. It was a nice dream, but the way my phone was already blowing up made it clear that was impossible.

Kids I didn't even know were texting me and sending me messages on social media. I ignored them all and focused on the text from Lacey.

Lacey: *I just heard the news and can't believe it. Grant is Kingsly? Are you okay?*

Me: *Yeah. I mean, I'm a little pissed, but I'm okay.*

Lacey: *Sorry about the competition! Gigi texted me the results. Want me to come over tonight? I can spend the night and we can trash talk Todd and Grant.*

Me: *LOL. Thanks, Lace. Not tonight. But that sounds perfect in a day or two.*

Lacey: *You got it. Call me if you need to talk tonight. I'll be by tomorrow.*

We stopped by the HEB close to home. Gigi ran in and bought me my favorite Bluebell ice cream. She said ice cream didn't solve problems but it sure did make a girl feel better while she was thinking about them. It was definitely the perfect night to shove my face in a pint of Butter Crunch.

Gigi dropped Lolli and me off at home, but wrapped me up in a big hug before she left.

"I know you're hurting, baby girl, but you're going to be okay. Sometimes things happen for a reason, only you may not find out the reason for days or months or even years. Have faith, baby. You're strong as steel and you are loved."

"Thanks, Gigi."

Lolli and I stood on the porch, watching Gigi drive off until her tail lights disappeared.

"She's right. You'll get through this, Bernie." Lolli took my hand and gave it a squeeze. "Would you like to watch some TV? It might help take your mind off of today."

"Thanks, Lolli, but I'm going to sit in the garage and eat this whole pint of ice cream."

"Then you'll need this…" Lolli opened the purse hanging on her forearm, reached in and handed me over a spoon.

"You carry a spoon in your purse?"

"You'd be surprised how many spoon emergencies crop up," she said. "I'll be watching TV in the family room…if you need to talk…or just a hug."

"Okay." I stepped off the porch with my pint of ice cream and escaped to the garage and the solitude I'd been needing since the news broke at the end of the competition.

Grant was Kingsly. How was that even possible?

Throwing myself on the loveseat, I proceeded to set a new Guinness Book World Record for fastest ice cream eating while juggling emotions. For the first time ever, my grandma Gigi was wrong. Because I didn't feel better while eating the ice cream. That didn't stop me from finishing it though, but it didn't help at all.

After tossing the empty pint in the trash, I paced in the space in front of Earl, but the more I looked at Earl, the more memories of me and Grant working, laughing, talking bubbled up and that invisible hand reached out and grabbed my lungs again.

I was confused, angry, sad, heartbroken and feeling more alone than ever before. Desperately needing some connection, I dragged the cover off the Mustang and slid into the driver's seat.

"Mama, I really need you right now." I gripped the steering wheel in both hands. "I've been trying to stay strong for dad, but right now I feel like dandelion fluff in a hurricane. I'm lost. So, so lost…Which is ridiculous because yesterday I knew where I was. At least I thought I did."

This wasn't working. I needed music. I turned the key but the battery was dead. Not a problem. I jumped out of the car and lifted the battery charger from the back shelf. I raised Tammi's hood to connect the charger and froze at what I saw. Sitting on top of the 302 Cubic Inch V-8 Engine was a faded pink envelope with my name in Mama's flowery script... *Bernadette.*

When I finally caught my breath, I picked it up and slid back behind the Mustang's steering wheel and opened it with shaking hands.

To my baby girl,

Your brothers will have received their letters. Right after my death. But you are so very young. So instead, my hope is that you're finding this a few years later. Maybe even exactly when you need to.

First, I want you to know how very hard I fought to live. You, your brothers, your father, and your grandmas mean everything to me. But life isn't fair. Sometimes life doesn't turn out the way we want. So I find strength in the fact that I married an amazing man who is an amazing father. It won't be easy, but your daddy will be the rock for each of you to hold on to.

And you have your brothers. They'll watch out for you. Even when you insisted on tagging along everywhere they went and you pestered them to no end—they looked out for their baby sister. Of course, they teased you to no end too, so it was a hard-earned tradeoff. I find comfort in knowing how much you love each other. How strong you'll be together.

I'm so sorry I will not get to see you grow up as I so want to.
I won't be able to drop you off on your first day of high school.
I won't be able to help you dress for your first date.
Or hug you in my arms when your heart hurts.
Or cheer when you graduate.
But I'll be there.
I will be there for every minute, my darling girl.

I ask a special favor...Please watch out for Grandma Lolli. I worry about her the most. I am her only child and this will be so very hard for her. She and I are close. We're much alike. We'd have our girls' day out in the city where we'd shop, stop in at the tea shop, and talk about "Project Runway" while we got our nails done. We made the mistake of including you once.

Do you remember? You ended up so bored you rearranged a window display, getting us all kicked out of the dress store. Lolli was embarrassed and I pretended to be, but you were quite creative. Needless to say your brothers gave you high-fives, but after that we let you stay home when Lolli & I had our girl time. Be patient with her and maybe give her an extra hug whenever you can. You girls will need to stick together.

In life, many people will say you cannot do things. Don't listen. You can do anything you set your mind to. Surround yourself with people who believe in you.

And finally... Thank you for being you, Bernie. Having you as my
daughter is one of the greatest joys of my life. Enjoy your life.

Don't rush it, baby girl. I will be waiting.
All my love, always,
Mama

Oh, my soul had needed this more than I'd known. I don't know how long I sat there with tears falling down my cheeks and my heart breaking for Mama...and me...and Lolli. Oh, my poor grandma Lolli.

Was Lolli feeling as lost as I felt right now? I'd spent so many years trying to be strong so no one had to worry about me—but I'd failed to see what was right in front of me. That Grandma Lolli was hurting. Was her obsession about the pageant simply her way to stay connected to Mama? The only way she knew to reach out to me?

I dried my face, stored Mama's letter safely in the glove compartment and went in the house to find Grandma Lolli.

"Lolli, can we talk?"

My grandma went still for a moment, then set down her cup of tea with a sigh.

"You're pulling out of the pageant," she said.

"No, I—"

"I understand, Bernie. I've been thinking it over, and it was wrong of me to force you to do it. I'm sorry, sweetie."

"I agree. It was wrong of you to force me. But I don't want to pull out. Actually, I came to ask you for help."

"What? Help?" Lolli sat up in her wingback chair. "You need my help?'

"Big time. My dress is all wrong. And my interview outfit, too. I could really use your help. Would you...go shopping with me?"

Grandma Lolli's face lit up with a wide, wobbly smile. "I'd love to. If you're free tomorrow, we can head into the city. There are some adorable boutiques your mama and I used to love."

"Perfect."

22

SHE DOESN'T KNOW SHE'S DATING A MOVIE STAR?

Grant

"King! You're finally back!" Frank, my agent, sat at the top of the conference table. "What do you have to say for yourself?"

What did I have to say? I looked around the table at my team —the team my parents and I had gathered together and had been carefully guiding my career for years and guilt twisted my stomach. Yeah, I owed them an explanation.

"First off, I apologize. I try not to make your jobs harder and definitely try not to act like a prima donna... But it looks like I went and did it anyway." I ran a hand around the back of my neck. "I was just trying to live a normal life for the first time ever. Obviously, I didn't think it through. It was selfish of me to think I could have my career and a taste of normalcy too. I'm truly sorry. The last thing I wanted to do was attract bad press.

"Now that the tabloids are in a frenzy over this story, you all know I've been a student at Jackson High School for the past three weeks. I played goalie, very badly. I entered an auto shop competition, and I lost that also. Stu, I'm sorry to say I ate junk food the whole time. Not one vegetable in three weeks. I forgot how good sugar and carbs taste." My gaze landed on Alison who wore a knowing smile. "Alison…"

"I already know." She lifted her hand in the air with a stop motion. "You didn't do a single work out. I figured it out by the third day, but I was enjoying your creativity. Except the day I worried someone might have a heart attack. Some of those workouts were pretty hilarious and a few were even impressive."

Right. Dax and TJ were better athletes than I was.

"It's not that I'm not grateful for everything all of you do for me. I am. In fact, I thank God every day that I have you guys on my team." I looked down at my shoes, thinking of just the right words to express what I'd been trying to do. "I just wanted to be a normal kid. That's all."

When I looked back up, I didn't see the expressions of frustration and anger that I was expecting. In fact, the closer I looked the more I realized everyone was pretty darn happy.

"Why don't you guys seem mad at me?"

"Maybe because you're one of the nicest, least ego-fueled actors we work with. Some actors trash hotel rooms, crash million dollar sports cars, or run up hundreds of thousands in gambling debts when they need a break." Frank leaned back in his chair, his arms behind his head with his elbows splayed out to the side and grinned. "You? You sign up for high school classes, join the varsity lacrosse team, and enter a statewide competition. Every one of us would be proud to have you as our own son."

"He's right." Donna nodded. "But we're also not mad because of all the free publicity."

"What publicity?"

"I guess you haven't been following the papers for the last three weeks," Frank said.

"Other than a few tabloid rumors, but those are always

crazy." I shrugged. "I wanted four King-free weeks. I've been busy with teenager stuff. Why? What did I miss?"

"Only the biggest free publicity campaign that every director and movie studio dreams of." Donna opened her laptop, brought up a few pages and passed the computer down to me.

I sat at the other end of the table to look.

"It started with the first 'Where's King?' headline in *The Tattler*. Other tabloids jumped in. Then your fan club started the "Where in the world is King?" contest and it exploded from there. Radio stations, *Entertainment Tonight*, and *Variety* all ran stories. It's gone global."

"That would explain some of the gossip going around school."

"The studio wanted to capitalize on it, so they brought Talia in on it. A few interviews of your worried girlfriend with close-ups of her beautiful tear-filled brown eyes really ratcheted up the air time we got."

"Wait, wait. Talia did an interview saying she was my girlfriend?"

"She was great. We figured you wouldn't mind since you two are such great friends. She's got a movie coming out next month, so the publicity helped her too."

I sat back and closed my eyes wondering how long that would take to get to Bernie.

"What's wrong, King? We thought you'd love the publicity—especially since you didn't have to do anything."

"What's wrong is I sort of have a real girlfriend." Have. Had. It was yet to be determined as I hadn't talked to Bernie yet. I had called and texted her more than a few times since Saturday with no response. Today was Monday and I felt like I was going to lose it. If I didn't hear from her today, I'd call Grady to make sure everything was okay.

"Congratulations!" Alison said.

"Well, it isn't official. Yet. I hadn't asked her, but we'd been on three dates and spent the past three weeks together. I was going to ask her. After I told her who I was."

"*What?* She doesn't know she's dating Kingsly Grant, the movie star?"

"She didn't. She found out on Saturday."

"And now she might think you're dating Talia? Oh, boy." Donna bit her lip. "That's not good. The poor girl."

"She'll think you're a liar and a two-timing cheating movie star," Stu said, adding to the twenty pound weight on my chest. "Like you were just playing with her."

"I know. She was already mad when she found out I was King."

"What kind of girl would be mad to find out the guy she's dating is a world-famous actor?"

"My kind of girl," I said. I pulled out my phone and brought up the video clip of the first time I'd seen Bernie. The one where the reporter was interviewing her in shop class. "You guys have actually seen her."

I hit play and turned my phone around for them to watch.

"So, I guess you're excited about the news." The reporter shifted the microphone back in front of Bernie.

"What news?" Bernie brushed a loose curl of chestnut hair from her cheek, leaving a streak of grease behind. *"If you're about to tell me the school board is finally going to fund more vocational training in schools, then yes. Very excited."*

"Oh, no. I was referring to the news about Kingsly Grant." Ms. Reed flashed Bernie a wide smile.

"Who's Kingsly Grant?"

"Uh... He's the hottest young actor in Hollywood right now."

"Oh, right. I think my friend Lacey made me go see one of his movies," Bernie said, not looking very excited about me or my movie.

The reporter frowned but plowed on. "Is it exciting to think he may choose your school to film his next movie?"

"Exciting?" Bernie shrugged, her gaze shifting to the undercarriage of the car. I grinned, now that I knew she really would rather be under her car working than talking about some movie star. *"Why? Pretty sure he puts his perfectly faded, over-priced designer jeans on the same as everyone else."*

The clip ended and everyone sat back, understanding my problem.

"Trust me when I say, Bernie is the last girl who would be impressed by a celebrity."

"Your Bernie is kick-ass," Donna said. "I thought so the first time I saw that clip."

"I'm sorry about the Talia thing, King." Frank looked heartsick over it. "I'd be happy to talk with her and explain, if you think that would help."

"Thanks. I'll let you know." I pushed from the table, deciding to ask my mom what she thought. I'd call her when I got home since she was still in Texas packing up the rental house. Once the paparazzi had descended on the tech competition, mom had driven me straight to the airport. Heading back to L.A. was the only way to get the paparazzi to head out too. "I'll catch you all later."

"Whoa, whoa, whoa." This came from Stu. "Let's talk food before you go. You do have a movie to film soon."

"Right." I grinned and patted my belly. "I'm back on the Stu train as of yesterday."

Alison pointed a finger to her chest. "And…?"

"And we're back to our regular workout schedule."

"Regular?" She lifted an eyebrow. "You'll need two-a-days for a while."

"Already on my schedule. It was totally worth it, by the way."

"We know, King." Frank, Donna, Alison, and Stu all smiled at me. "You deserved that time. We're happy for you."

It took me an hour and a half to drive home through L.A.'s heavy traffic, but I listened to the Motown playlist I'd downloaded onto my phone and thought about something from the auto tech competition that had been bugging me. I was still trying to figure out how we lost.

Something had happened at the end. I remembered Bernie seemed preoccupied. I recalled the last RO I had run to the parts counter. I'd been distracted at the time watching the paparazzi file in with dread. As soon as I focused my mind on the repair order in my hand, I saw it in my mind. The 3-Cs were listed, but she hadn't filled them in. And like she'd told me the 3-Cs were worth most of the points. There was no way she forgot them. No way.

So the question was… Why would Bernie throw the competition?

After I'd eaten a chicken Caesar salad big enough to satiate a Hobbit, I settled onto my patio overlooking the city and called Mom.

"Mom, I need your advice." I cut right to the chase. "Bernie won't respond to my texts or calls. I need to talk to her."

"I'm sure you do. But maybe think about what she needs," Mom said.

"An apology."

"Yes, but she needs a little time first. Heck, Grant, she thought she was dating some sweet nerd and in the middle of her worst moment—she found out you weren't who she thought you were."

"I know. I know. I didn't mean for anything to work out that way. And that's not even the worst. Frank and Donna told me they turned my being missing into a big PR deal and even brought in Talia as the worried girlfriend."

"Oh, poor Bernie. I can't imagine how she'll feel if she hears that."

And she would. Some kid like Todd or some mean girl would be sure to tell her.

"I didn't mean to hurt her. I really like her, Mom."

"I picked up on that." I heard the smile in my mom's voice. "The other thing to think about is how it feels to her. You two lost the competition, then suddenly you're not Grant, but King —and then you left town. From her perspective it might feel like she never mattered. Like you never really cared."

"Shoot. That couldn't be further from the truth."

"Then maybe you should tell her that."

"She won't talk to me."

"That's why you'll need to show her."

Show her. Yes. I needed to show Bernie how I felt. But how?

23

GIRL TIME

Bernie

"What do you need the most help with?" Lolly sat across from me at our kitchen table. The soft smile on her face and twinkle in her eyes helped me know I made the right decision.

"Almost everything." I took a quick bite of my blueberry pancake and washed it down with some milk. "The dress, makeup, my hair, practicing for the interview. Basically, Lolli, I need a lot of help."

"You'll be fine. We'll head over to Red Oaks and go to the cute little boutique your mama and I used to go to. You don't need much makeup, so that's really not a problem. My beauty parlor is closed on Sundays, but I'll call LuAnn tomorrow and see if she can fit you in this week." She slid another pancake onto my plate. "If you want, we can even get your nails done."

My nails? My knee-jerk reaction was to turn her down. I'd never had my nails done. It wasn't something I wanted or needed. It was also totally impractical for a girl who worked on cars.

"I haven't gone since the last time your mama and I went."

Lolli's eyes went soft and watery but she blinked a few times, gathering herself together.

"I'd love to." I could kick myself for not having figured out how badly Lolli was hurting. *Thanks, mama. Thanks for helping me see.* I promised myself right then and there that I wouldn't complain once this week.

"Anybody home?" Lacey entered through the side kitchen door.

"Good morning, Lacey. You're just in time to go dress shopping with us," Lolli said. "Bernie and I could use your help."

I nodded. "Yeah. I could use all the help I can get."

"I need to tell you something first." Lacey bit her lip. "You may not want to talk to me after I tell you this."

"Tell me what?"

"Grady told me this morning that he knew who Grant was the whole time." Lacey paused and huffed out of breath. "He did say he warned Grant—*King*—not to get involved with you if he wasn't serious. I'm just so mad at both of them right now I could scream. I'm sorry. I wish Grady had told me so I could've warned you. I will totally understand if you don't want me to go shopping with you. And you can even be mad at me for a little bit. Just not for too long because you're my best friend."

"I'm not mad at you at all. This isn't your fault." I tried to think it over but everything was still too new and too raw. "I doubt I'm mad at Grady either, but I reserve the right to change my mind about that."

"Oh, thank goodness because I would hate it if you were mad at me. Especially because you know how much I like dress shopping." Lacey sat at the table next to me and grabbed my hand. "But that's not all... I was on one of the online Hollywood gossip sites last night, and they had an interview with King's girlfriend—Talia West, the actress. That fake adorable nerd is a two-timing, lying Hollywood jerk."

Ooookay. That hurt and I didn't even know who Talia West

160

was. But I guess it cleared everything up, didn't it? Now I knew everything between us was a lie. What was I? Research? A joke? Was he laughing behind my back the whole time?

I pictured his face. His wild blond hair and lopsided smile. His dark brown eyes, so warm and sincere.

"Hey—I know why *I* didn't recognize him, but how is it that people who know who Kingsly Grant is, didn't recognize him?"

"Contacts," Lacey growled. "King has the lightest blue eyes. So light they almost glow. And that ratfink nerd wore—"

"Dark brown contacts." Right. Those dark brown eyes I fell for were fake.

I recalled the times we talked about our childhoods and about feeling like we didn't fit in...about liking each other... And the sad thing was none of it *felt* fake. All of those moments...all of those conversations—they felt real and honest. It was all so darn confusing.

"You know what? I'm not gonna worry about it. It's over. I have better things to do than worry about Grant Stutterfield. And that other guy—Kingsly Grant—I don't even know him. I refuse to waste my time on him."

That sounded braver and more self-assured than I felt, but I could deal with it later. I had something much more important to do.

"Who's ready to go shopping?" I cleared our plates to the sink and grabbed my car keys. "If finding the dress doesn't take too long, Lolli, maybe we can stop at that tea place you and Mama used to go to."

Lolli smiled. "That sounds lovely."

* * *

Between school and working on pageant stuff with Lolli and Lacey it was a week of highs and lows:

The highs—and I would've bet money I never would've said

this in my entire life—were the shopping trips (it took more than one to find a dress all three of us liked) and the hair appointment and the nail salon visit (I compromised with a clear coat) with Lolli and Lacey.

The lows—you can imagine the lows at school. (Tomboy gets punked by famous hot movie star and then deserted for his supermodel girlfriend.) Trust me when I say some kids at school enjoyed my situation and were happy to talk about it—to me, in front of me, or behind my back.

* * *

And then the week finally ended and it was Saturday, the night of the pageant.

Lolli, Gigi, and Lacey drove with me to the pageant. *Roll Tide*. No, I wasn't an Alabama fan; it was just something my sport-obsessed brothers always said before a big game. Now that I understood why it was so important to Lolli—it felt like a big game.

"I'm going to hang up your gown in the dressing room back stage and check out the competition," Lacey said and left before I could tell her not to worry about the competition.

Gigi just laughed because she wasn't a pageant girl either.

"Bernadette, no matter what happens tonight, this week has been a gift." Lolli took my hands and squeezed. "Thank you for putting up with me."

"I had fun, too. I love you, Lolli. I'm happy to follow in yours and mama's footsteps. But I'm relieved you don't care about me winning. Because that will never happen. Especially because I sort of changed my talent."

"Oh, thank goodness." She flashed me a relieved smile. "I didn't want to say anything, but your accordion playing is atrocious. Now, I'm going to get us good seats down in front."

She rushed off more excited than I'd seen her in maybe ever.

I turned a knowing eye to Grandma Gigi who stood there looking oh-so-innocent. Yeah, I wasn't buying it.

"You knew. That's why you traded turns with Lolli. You knew Lolli needed help."

"I knew you both needed help." Gigi reached out her palm and cupped my cheek. "Help I couldn't give you. You two had to help each other."

"Yeah, we did."

Lacey came running over from somewhere backstage looking wild-eyed.

"So, I have good news and bad news." She placed a bracing hand on my shoulder. "Which would you like first?"

"The good news."

"You know that perfect dress we spent three days looking for and it looks amazing on you? Well, some girl with big hair and a snotty nose just puked on it."

"How is that good news?" I asked, grossed out about throw-up on my turquoise gown.

"The vomit only landed on the bottom part of the dress, so I cut the dress which means, you'll be wearing a mini-skirt dress which is great because you've got amazing legs."

Oh boy.

"I'm afraid to hear the bad news now."

"It's bad. I just heard the MC say they got a celebrity to announce the winner."

"Please don't tell me it's—"

"Kingsly Grant. They got Kingsly Grant."

Drat. And I thought vomit on my dress was bad.

I was so not ready to deal with the world-famous movie star hiding out as an adorable fake nerd who had pretended to like me so he could research his next role.

Grandma Gigi grinned at me.

"I know, Gigi." I sucked in a breath and put on my mental armor. "Sometimes you've got to live through an experience in order to learn life's greatest lessons."

24

WHO WROTE THIS SCRIPT?

Grant

Have you ever had a jolt of intuition that you must do something, or else? You know, like a gut feeling that if you didn't do this thing...

I'd only had this spark of intuition happen *three* other times in my life.

The first two times were life-changing. The first time—and the best—was when my parents asked if I'd like to be adopted and become a part of their family. The second time was when I was offered my first movie role—one so small that other actors had turned it down—yet that had been the role that catapulted me from TV to movie star.

The third time...well, it was still undecided, but looking doubtful.

Now, this fourth jolt of intuition—the one telling me to get the heck out of here before Bernie saw me—might be my most prescient jolt ever. Yet, I couldn't do a thing about it.

The studio had set this up. They wanted to keep the "Where in the World is Kingsly Grant?" momentum going. That's how I ended up sitting in this small Texas auditorium waiting to crown this year's winner of the Miss Armadillo Pageant.

Who wrote this script? Not me.

This was definitely not how I wanted to see Bernie for the first time since she found out who I was. I'd been stuck in L.A. taking care of necessary meetings and public appearances all week, so my only chance to explain everything and apologize to Bernie had been through texts and phone calls.

Too bad she'd blocked me.

I had to fly back to L.A. tonight for one more week of obligations before I could come back here. My hope was that these two weeks would give Bernie space to see the good things we had and let go of her anger. I was still trying to figure out a good way to *show* Bernie how I felt.

Since I was hiding out up in the lighting booth until it was time to crown the winner, I had an eagle-eye view of the pageant. First up was the evening gown competition. All twenty girls walked across the stage, one at a time, striking a pose in the center before spinning once and then taking their place in line upstage. There were the typical rhinestone-studded sparkling gowns with mermaid trains, some with layer upon layer of ruffles, a few with skirts covered in downy faux feathers. There was one contestant in a mini dress and I knew by her lose-limbed athletic walk it was Bernie. The mini skirt was a surprise, but she had long athletic legs, so maybe Lacey had talked her into it.

Next came the interviews. Each contestant was called down-stage to talk with the Master of Ceremonies. The MC asked each contestant the same question: why is your platform impor-tant to you?

There were girls with platforms for world peace, women's rights, anti-bullying, literacy, the need for vocational training in schools and others. All great. Guess which one was Bernie's?

Everyone needs a skilled mechanic or plumber or electrician they can count on. Over in Germany, they respect blue-collar jobs and sixty percent of their high school graduates choose vocational training. But here in America, our public high schools continue to cut vocational training from curriculums. We look down on blue collar work and push every high school student toward college. One third of all college students drop out entirely without a degree and burdened with student loan debt. Yet there is a growing shortage of skilled labor and millions of jobs going unfilled. Who are you going to call if a pipe bursts in your house or your daughter's car breaks down on the side of the road? That's why I believe vocational training is important.

Good answer, right? I loved everything about this girl. Except that she was too stubborn to talk to me. But I was working on that.

Next up was the talent. This would be interesting because the last time I'd heard Bernie practice her song on the accordion, it sounded like a cat fight after the cats had swallowed harmonicas. Painfully bad.

But before Bernie's turn there was a baton twirler, a piano solo, a reading from Romeo and Juliet, more than a few tap dances, a lot of solos including a gutsy performance of "Defying Gravity," and then Bernie was up.

I sat up straight when she entered the stage without her accordion and wheeling out a large, tarp-covered object.

Bernie raised her hand to quiet the polite applause and cleared her throat nervously.

"I was originally going to play a song on the accordion for you, but I'm against torture so decided against it. Instead, I'm going to demonstrate how to quickly change a flat tire." She pulled the tarp off to reveal a tire attached to a wheel on a stand. She had the spare tire and her tool box hanging on the back side of her stand. "Emphasis on quickly. I believe strongly this is a skill everyone should know for their own safety."

With a nod to the sound man in the booth, her music (The William Tell Overture) started and Bernie was off and running. Her movements were precise and confident. So smooth it could have been done by a professional NASCAR pit crew. She pried off the hubcap, loosened the lug nuts, jacked the tire up off the ground, removed the lug nuts, hoisted the tire off, replacing it with the spare and then did it all in reverse, finishing before the music did.

"That's all there is to it. Don't forget to check your tire pressure and rotate them approximately every six-thousand miles. Thank you, and hug your mechanic!"

She got a loud round of applause as she left the stage. Maybe even the loudest of the night.

"While the judges tabulate their votes, let's bring all our contestants back out on stage. Come on out, ladies!" The girls reentered dressed again in their gowns, lining up behind the MC. Bernie slid into her place at the end a little after the rest since she had the least time to change. "Let's give them all one more round of applause, shall we?"

The crowd clapped and whistled.

"We'd like to introduce our special guest tonight. Ladies and gentlemen, all the way from Hollywood…"

Whoops. I'd been so busy watching Bernie, I'd forgotten they wanted me in the wings right after the talent. I told the sound guy to have the MC stall for a few minutes and rushed out of the booth, down the stairwell, weaving my way through the corridor to the stage door while I slid on my suit jacket and straightened my tie.

I nodded to the stage hand, who whispered into the mic attached to the earpiece in the MC's ear that I was ready.

"It's an honor and a thrill to introduce actor Kingsly Grant all the way from Hollywood to crown this year's Miss Armadillo! Kingsly Grant, everyone!"

I stepped into the spotlight to huge applause and screaming

girls, but all I could think about was Bernie standing behind me. If this were an action-adventure movie, I'd swing onto the stage on a rope, scoop her up, and climb up onto the lighting catwalk, holding her hostage until she gave me a chance to explain.

Once again, I had to remind myself life wasn't a movie. No happy endings guaranteed.

"Judges, do you have the envelope?" The MC leaned down, accepting the envelope from a matronly woman in a pink chiffon gown. "Last year's reigning Miss Armadillo, Bobbi Jo Isles, will be helping King make the presentations. Here we go…"

Bobbi Jo handed me a bouquet of flowers and a small silver trophy of an armadillo.

"Our second runner up is…Wendy Bosch! Congratulations, Wendy!"

Wendy stepped forward as the other contestants congratulated her and the audience cheered.

A quick glance at Bernie showed happy relief, which made me want to laugh, but I quickly moved to hand an excited Wendy her flowers and trophy.

"Congratulations, Wendy." I bent and bussed her cheeks like we do in Hollywood and France.

"The first runner up is…Elena Ruiz! Everyone put your hands together for Elena!"

I handed Elena her trophy and flowers, but before I could bend down for the cheek kisses, she squealed and threw her arms around me with an "I love you, King!"

I laughed and extricated myself, moving back to get the crown for the winner.

"Here we go. The moment we've been waiting for. This year's Miss Armadillo is…Bernadette Jewell!"

"Wait, what?" Bernie said, looking like they'd just announced her name in the Hunger Games lottery on reaping day. She was so shocked (possibly appalled) that the other girls had to push her out to the center of the stage while people laughed and cheered.

That's my girl. Only she wasn't.

"Congratulations, Bernadette."

"Don't even start," she growled at me. "Just do your movie star part and slap the crown on my head, okay?'

Ooookay. So she was still angry with me. Understandable.

I placed the crown on her head while she avoided looking into my eyes. When I leaned in for the cheek kisses, she stepped on my foot with the heel of her shoe. The *sharp* heel of her shoe. *Ow.*

But…it gave me hope. By my reasoning, she wouldn't be angry if she didn't care. I was going to cling to that while I figured out a way to show her how much she meant to me.

25

AN INTERVENTION

Bernie

"Grady says he thinks King really is a great guy." Lacey stood next to me as I attached a bolt in the Mustang.

"Then tell Grady to date him."

"Sorry, Grady's already taken. It's my job as your best friend to tell you that you're being stubborn and bratty."

"I know I am. Why do you think I'm hiding out here by myself in the garage?" I puffed out a breath, attempting to get a loose curl off my face. "So I don't have to make anybody else suffer until I'm through this."

"You've been out here almost a week. How much more time do you need?"

"I don't know. Six months. Maybe a year." How long did broken hearts take to heal? The garage had once again become my refuge. Only this time, instead of working on Earl, Tammi was saving me.

Tammi had gone from being hidden under the tarp for years to being my touchstone; the place I'd go to talk to Mama. For years, I would buy a part for the Mustang when I felt the loss of my mother too keenly.

Things had changed.

Now, instead of buying parts—I was installing parts when I felt the sharp loss of Grant. The loss of what we had together. The loss of the future I sort of thought we'd have. I mean, who says he's planning a fourth date if he doesn't mean it?

"Okay. That's it. Let's go." Lacey took the wrench from my hand, tossed it into the tool box and dragged me from the garage and into the house. "It's time for an intervention."

"You're not serious," I said.

"I absolutely am. First, we're watching a Kingsly Grant movie and you will sit here and watch."

"Lace, I don't care that he's a famous actor."

"That's not the point. You know how you're good with cars?"

I raised an eyebrow at her and crossed my arms over my chest.

"Stop. You are. Just because your sensitive side—shut up, you have one—felt sorry for Todd and you threw the competition doesn't mean you aren't a great tech. Now say it: I'm a great tech."

"You're a great tech." I snickered when Lacey frowned. Hey, I thought it was funny. "Okay, I'm a great tech."

"Right. Well, guess what? Grant is a great actor. He's really good at his job."

"Yes, I know. I had a front-row seat to his performance. Remember?"

"Sit down, be quiet and watch." Lacey waited for me to sit before she sat next to me and clicked on the TV and one of his movies.

It only took one movie to see what Lacey was saying. Kingsly Grant was an amazing actor. Of course, first I had to get over seeing him with blue eyes. The lightest blue eyes I'd ever seen. They were beautiful and breathtaking. His long hair was gone too, cut short like some Navy Seal which he had the body for, too. Weird to think he hid that muscled body under his baggy "cool kid" hoodie and other nerd outfits for three weeks.

Lacey hit pause when the credits rolled on the screen. "Well?"

"He's an amazing actor. I'm still not sure what the point of this is." That wasn't true. I figured Lacey knew that the longer I watched King on TV, the deeper I'd fall for him. I narrowed my eyes on her, realizing she was as diabolical as Lolli when she wanted something. "Ha! You're Lolli right now and Kingsly Grant is a blueberry pancake. He still lied to me."

"I was prepared for you to say that. Not the pancake part, but come on." Lacey pulled me up and walked me back into the kitchen. "Welcome to Intervention Part Two."

Lacey wasn't kidding about the intervention. This wasn't some impromptu idea. She'd planned this ahead of time. Lolli, Gigi, and Grant's mom were all sitting around the kitchen table waiting for us. *They had snacks.* Which meant they were serious.

"Hello, Mrs. Stutterfield—I mean, Mrs. Grant," I said, giving Lacey serious side-eye about her inclusion.

"Please, call me April. Don't blame Lacey, dear. I wanted to help," she said, sending me a smile. "And I've never been part of an intervention before, and Lacey made it sound like so much fun."

"Yay." Fun for who? I sat at the table ready to get this over with. "So, just so we're all on the same page, so far we've established that Kingsly is an amazing actor—which I already knew without watching one of his movies. He lied to me about who he is, and he's had a girlfriend the whole time he pretended to like me. I'm aware that I'm being very bratty—sorry. As soon as I work through this anger, I'll stop. Or at least, that's my plan."

"I don't blame you one bit, Bernie. I'd be angry and hurt too if some movie star came along, flirted with me and didn't tell me about his girlfriend."

"You would?"

"Yes. Absolutely. If it were true...which in Grant's case—it isn't. He and Talia grew up in the industry together. We're friends with her parents. They're like brother and sister. The studio didn't know about you—so when the story about Kingsly being missing caught fire, they saw it as free publicity. And asked Talia to play the worried girlfriend. She didn't know about you either, or she wouldn't have done it."

Hmmm. Lacey nudged her elbow into my arm and nodded at me.

"I told you Grady said he thought Grant was too nice to do that."

"He should've told you who he was, but he didn't mean to hurt you, Bernie." April pushed the plate of cookies toward me. "Coming to Texas—trying to live a regular life like a regular teenager—was about having people like him for himself instead of his celebrity. That's what you gave him, Bernie. He's rarely had that. It meant so much to him that he was afraid to ruin it."

"But he *knew* me. He should've trusted me."

"Did he tell you about his brother?" April asked.

"A little. He said his younger brother was adopted by a different family. And that he finally met him but it didn't go very well. That's all he said."

"Grant wanted to find his brother since the first day we brought him home. It took years to track him down and get his brother's family to agree to meet. You probably already know that Grant has a huge heart. He was sure that finding his brother would fill a hole in his heart. But once his brother realized who Grant was, he was resentful. Angry over the life Grant had compared to the life he had."

"That's ridiculous," Lacey said.

"I agree. Still, he asked Grant for money and other things and Grant gave it to him because he loved his brother. But his brother never loved him. It was all about what Grant could give him and being seen in public with Grant. Eventually it caused

Grant more pain than he could handle, so he walked away. When you're a celebrity, being used for your fame and fortune isn't new. But he thought it was going to be different with his brother."

"Oh, man." That explained the pain in his eyes when he mentioned that it hadn't gone the way he'd hoped.

"The poor boy," Lolli said, reaching out and patting April's hand.

"I think it's why he went to such great lengths to make sure the next important person in his life, liked him for himself."

"Now hold on," Gigi said. "That timeline doesn't make sense. He came here incognito before he knew Bernie. So how did he know to go to such great lengths?"

Yeah. Everyone's gazes whipped over to April.

"That's not exactly true," she said. "Bernie applied for a grant from Grant's charity foundation. When he read it, the letter reminded him of his own passion and drive. He was intrigued by a girl mechanic. The fact that you asked for funds for your school and not yourself impressed both of us. Grant fell for Bernie before he ever met her."

"He came to Texas and Jackson High to meet Bernie?" Lacey sighed. "That is so romantic. It's like a movie."

"You know, Bernie." Lolli looked at me and smiled. "Most movies have happy endings."

Did they?

26

GRANT, EARL, TAMMI & MARVIN

Bernie

I woke up tired the next morning since I could hardly sleep that night. Every time I'd close my eyes I'd see Grant. Grant laughing in my garage. Grant surfing like some hot god on the TV screen. Grant snitching my lunch. Grant putting everything he had into learning about cars—for me.

After throwing on jeans and a T-shirt for school, I reached for my phone to call Gigi to talk it over, but stopped before making the call. I didn't need to call Gigi. She didn't need to be my only lifeline anymore.

I grabbed my boots and headed into the kitchen.

"Hey, Lolli? What do you think Mama would do if she were in my shoes?"

"Your mama was a true romantic, so my guess is if she were in your shoes, she'd be on the first plane to California to go after that boy."

"It's one of my options."

"I'm happy to hear that," Lolli said. "Just a heads up, I'm having the garage fumigated for termites, so it'll be off limits for a few days."

Ugh. There went my escape and stress release for a few days. Maybe I could take up boxing this week.

* * *

When I told Lacey I was thinking of flying out to L.A. to see Grant, she screamed so loudly that the teacher on duty in the cafeteria asked us to leave.

"*Yeeessss!* I knew you wouldn't let me down!"

"That's if I don't chicken out. I still have to get through the rest of this week."

Trust me when I say school had been no fun. Because everybody had found out that Grant was Kingsly Grant. And everybody had heard about his famous Hollywood girlfriend. A few kids made sure to tell me about his girlfriend—you know, in case I didn't know and so they could laugh at me. I thought I didn't fit in before, but now that I was the butt of everyone's jokes, I *really* didn't fit in.

Todd made auto shop class worse than usual. Although, maybe for the first time, I understood Todd. Kids who were bullied usually end up bullies themselves. Everything sort of fell into place after overhearing the way Todd's father treated him. I figured he was embarrassed, knowing I had heard his father screaming at him. Knowing I had seen the tears in his eyes. So I was willing to ignore his obnoxiousness for a few days.

I lasted a day. Because Todd had become even cockier pain-in-the butt Todd 2.0 since he beat me in the tech competition.

"Loser alert," Todd called as I walked into shop class. "Double loser between the competition and being dumped by a movie star. It must suck to be you, Bernard."

"Not as bad is it must suck to be you, Todd. You know what I just realized? I don't need to compete with you anymore. And it has nothing to do with feeling sorry for you. Because I don't. You're old enough to know how bad it feels to get bullied." I cocked an eyebrow at him. "Old enough to know that it sucks, yet you still do it to others. So, no. I don't need to compete with you, but I will call you out every time I see you bully someone in school. Every. Time."

I enjoyed seeing the smirk fall from his face.

By Thursday I was at the end of my rope. I ducked into a bathroom to escape for a few minutes. I needed a break. I needed time to regroup so I could go back out there and take more punishment.

Guess who was in the bathroom? Yeah, Breanna Smith and her mean girl posse.

"Look who it is! It's Kingsly Grant's reject." She laughed and her girls joined in. "How does it feel to be his little piece on the side?"

I wanted to turn around and walk right back out. I didn't. I straightened my spine and kept moving. But then the craziest thing happened.

"You know what's funny?" Breanna snorted. "You thought you could compete with Talia. She's, like, a supermodel."

That wasn't the crazy thing. The crazy thing was just as I was walking past them to wash my hands and ignore them the way I always did—I heard a voice in my head. Grant's voice telling me to stop fitting in. Telling me I wasn't the problem; it was them. And his voice stopped me in my tracks. I turned around and walked right up to Breanna, staring directly into her eyes.

"I'm not anyone's reject. And I don't need to compete because I'm the one who walked away. But I will share one thing…" I looked at her smirking face and let my lips slide into a big, slow smile. "Kingsly Grant is an amazing kisser. A-mazing."

That shut them all up. I won't lie; I enjoyed the looks of shock and envy on their faces as I turned and walked out of the bathroom.

A small victory in a week that felt like a battlefield.

"Hey, Bernie! Come quick!" Lacey was standing at the end of a hallway, waving her arm at me. "You're not going to believe this!"

"I don't know, Lace. It's been a heck of a week." In a bad way. I didn't think I could take anything more.

Lacey locked elbows with mine and walked me into the front foyer of the school where a large crowd was gathering and many students pushing through the series of doors to head outside.

"Let's go," Lacey said, heading us outside also. Even more kids were standing outside along with many of the teachers, secretaries and even Principal Barstow.

The crowd parted for us, clearing an opening like wind through a wheat field. That's when I almost fell over.

Because Kingsly Grant stood in front of a freshly painted Earl (Tahoe Turquoise!) and he held a boom box in his hands. As soon as his eyes met mine, he pushed the boom box on and held it over his head while he looked at me defiantly, unashamedly, and with a whole lot of something that made me go weak in the knees.

"Holy cow. He's recreating the *Say Anything* 'boom box' scene." Lacey put her hand over her mouth. "I'm really going to need Grady to do this for me. Although I don't recognize the song."

I did. "If I Could Build My Whole World Around You" by Tammi Terrell and Marvin Gaye. He was playing my favorite Motown song. For me. For us.

He held his hand out to me and I walked straight into his arms and kissed him.

Maybe people started cheering and whistling. Maybe that was fireworks exploding in my chest. Pretty sure I heard Principal Barstow call for all the students to get back inside. All I know is when we finally ran out of breath and Tammi and Marvin stopped singing, I pulled back and looked into the most beautiful blue eyes I'd ever seen.

"I'm sorry," Grant said. "I'm sorry I didn't trust you enough to tell you who I was sooner."

"It's okay." I lifted my hand to his jaw. "Your mom explained."

"I have to ask… Why did you throw the contest? I know you did. I saw the repair order. I don't understand why you would do that. It was so important to you. You studied so hard. We studied so hard so we could win this for you. What happened?"

"I realized that maybe Todd needed to win more than I did."

"What are you going to do? I thought you needed the scholarship money."

"I do, but it turns out the Miss Armadillo Pageant awarded scholarships. Who knew? So I have enough to cover my first semester."

"What about needing to prove to your boss that you're just as good a technician as a guy?"

"I thought a lot about that. I was frustrated about not fitting in in a guy's world. Angry that I had to jump through hoops that Todd or some other male mechanic didn't have to."

"That's not fair."

"Yeah, but someone recently reminded me that life isn't fair. It's not fair for anybody. Everybody has something that they have to deal with. Your mom gave you up and you had to watch your little brother get adopted before you. Not fair. I lost my mama, my dad lost the love of his life, and Lolli lost her daughter to cancer. None of that is fair.

"So instead of throwing a fit over life's unfairness, I have other options. There are all-female garages. Or maybe my dad and I will start a garage together. Or maybe I'll teach. I'll figure something out and I'll be okay."

"Yes, you will." He leaned down and kissed my forehead. "You amaze me."

"I know I'm not very girly and I have trouble expressing my emotions," I said. "But I feel so very lucky you came into my life."

"It was more than luck. I had this gut feeling if I didn't do this, I'd miss out on something important. Something I may never have gotten the chance at again."

"I get it. I do. This was your only chance to experience a normal life away from the spotlight."

"That's not it. I thought it was too—for a long time—but it's not. The important thing I would have missed out on—is meeting you."

Lolli was right. I'm more like Mama than I thought. Because my heart just went gooey like a marshmallow over a fire.

"Can we talk about Earl? Because he's beautiful! How did you sneak—" I blinked up at his smiling face. "Lolli helped you. She lied about the termite treatment."

"It's a grand gesture like in the movies. I was trying to show you how I felt about you."

"Thank you." I raised up on my toes and planted a kiss on his lips. "It love it."

"Two more things," Grant said. "First, I'd like to take you somewhere, but it's a surprise."

"You know how I am with surprises—especially after the last one."

"Hey, it turned out okay in the end, right?" Grant hit me with his bluer-than-blue gaze and every cell in my body gave a thumbs up.

"True. I trust you, so okay, but if it's Burger Barn, I want a tray of tots all for myself."

"So noted." He laughed, but got serious right away. "Second, I'd like to make this official. What I'm saying is, Bernadette, will you be my girlfriend?"

"You're going to cost me money, Kingsly Grant." *The boyfriend bet.* "But I'd love to be your girlfriend."

Grant smiled and leaned down and kissed me. "I'll try to make it worth it."

"You already did." *Worth every penny.*

EPILOGUE

Grant

Okay, I might have downplayed the surprise a bit, but I didn't want to freak Bernie out.

"You own a private jet?" Bernie had stopped on the tarmac. "I just assumed we'd, you know, be flying on a commercial flight."

"I don't own it. The studio rented it." I wrapped my arm around her shoulders to keep us moving to the plane and up the set of stairs.

We boarded, met the flight crew, and moved into the luxurious seating section to stow our bags and settle in.

"This is not good," Bernie said, buckling herself in while her head swiveled around taking it all in.

"Why isn't it good? I thought you'd like it." Technically, this was only our fourth date, so, of course, I was trying to impress Bernie.

"I've never flown before."

"Never?"

"Nope. So, it'll all be downhill from here." She grinned over at me. "I'm kidding, but this is impressive."

"But wait—there's more." I grabbed out the movies I'd stashed in my travel bag and held them up. "I've planned this date carefully. For our inflight entertainment, I thought we could watch a *Lord of the Rings* movie. But I brought the *Hobbit* movies also in case you need a refresher."

"Excuse me, what?" Bernie's eyes went wide and she reached out and took *The Fellowship of the Ring* from my hand. "*Movies?* They made the books into movies?"

"You didn't know? Of course, you didn't." I laughed. "How did a movie actor like me end up with a girl who hates movies?"

"I don't hate movies. I've just had…better things to do. Lacey forced me to watch another of your movies"—she darted her eyes to me and away—"and I get it."

"Get what?"

"Get why you're famous. You're a talented actor." She tilted her head and narrowed her eyes on me. "And I get the whole drooling female fans thing too. What I find amazing is that girls at Jackson didn't find awkward nerdy Grant as hot as I did."

"I only needed one girl at Jackson to find me hot, and you did."

We ended up watching most of *The Hobbit* (we decided to start chronologically) on the three hour flight to L.A.

Once we touched down, a limo waited to whisk us off.

The surprise? I had an awards show to attend and I wanted Bernie to walk the red carpet with me. Partly just because I loved spending time with Bernie, but also because I wanted to make it clear to all the kids at Jackson High and my fans that Bernie was my girl. She hadn't said anything, but Lacey had told me about how mean kids at school had been.

Lacey and Lolli had helped me with the surprise and had packed a simple sheath of a dress (not a single ruffle or bow) in Bernie's favorite Tahoe Turquoise and she looked gorgeous.

"This is crazy." Bernie leaned into me to hiss as the paparazzi and fans flashed their cameras and called our names (Yes, everyone knew who Bernie was.)

Crazy, yes, but it was my life. At some point along the red carpet, as I stopped again and again to get interviewed by reporters, I lost Bernie. Literally lost her. I turned around and she was gone. I twisted my head around, trying to catch a glimpse of her turquoise gown but there were so many glittery gowns it was impossible.

I'd just taken out my phone to call her when Lacey texted. She and Grady were over with Lolli & Gigi watching the awards show on television.

Lacey: *You totally lost our girl.*

Me: *I didn't lose her, I—did you see where she went?"*

I figured she wouldn't be busting my chops otherwise.

Lacey: *Go back to the street where the cars are arriving. Just saw her talking with that hot actor from Stranger Things about his car (Grant says it's a Lamborghini).*

Me: *Thanks! She looks beautiful, doesn't she?*

Lacey: *She does. Lolli & Gigi cried when they saw her on TV. Grady says you don't even look like a penguin in your tux (which is a compliment, I think.)*

Me: *Haha. I've got to go find my girlfriend.*

Sure enough, I found her. I knew Bernie had no idea the guy she was giving advice to— while they leaned over his engine— was one of the hot, up-and-coming actors up for best actor tonight.

Before I could even call her name, Bernie stood up straight and turned her head, looking right at me with a bright smile. It was like she sensed I was there. Which I found very cool. I figured she'd enjoy the cars more than the famous people.

Wait until I told her that the ABG Foundation had awarded the Devil's Lap County School System enough money to run vocational classes for the next five years.

Bernie had said she felt lucky that I'd come into her life.

It wasn't luck. It was pure intuition that guided us together.

Like I said, the *three* times I'd acted on my intuition…were *life-changing*. In the best way.

A NOTE FROM M.L.

Thank you for taking the time to read *THE TOMBOY & THE MOVIE STAR.* If you enjoyed it, it would be sweet if you have time to leave a review on Amazon. And I hope you'll stick around for the next installment in the Jackson High Series. Thank you! ♥ M.L.

HUGE HEARTFELT THANKS TO...

My readers! Thank you for loving the Jackson High Series! For loving quirky, sweet romances that make you snicker, swoon, and sigh.

To my amazing editors! You ladies are the bomb.

To my Beta readers for reading through my not-very-pretty rough drafts. But, hey, it's not like I forced you to listen to me sing.

To my proofreader, Mrs. "Eagle-Eyes" K. I couldn't have done this one without you. ;)

ABOUT M.L. COLLINS

M.L. Collins has done stuff. Good stuff. Bad stuff. Fun stuff. Boring stuff. She believes in true love, laughing loud and often, being kind, and assuming the best in people until they show you otherwise. She loves classic rock, old Motown, and '90s country music. She hates negative people, dill pickles, and scary movies. Loves windy days, dogs, and LOTR. She's an unashamed lover of sprinkles on cupcakes.

M.L. loves reading and writing quirky sweet romance novels that make you snicker, swoon, and sigh. She loves hearing from readers!

Printed in Great Britain
by Amazon

72282204R00116